More GEMS

More
GEMS

12-Step Shares,
Notes and Thoughts

Andy C.

ISBN: 9781990446177 (IS Paperback)

ISBN: 9781990446191 (IS Hardcover)

ISBN: 9781990446184 (KDP Print)

ISBN: 9781990446207 (Digital ePub)

ALSO BY THIS AUTHOR

GEMS

Still More GEMS

Closing Arguments for 12-Stepping Lawyers

You can find Andy C at the4thdimension.ca

Contents

Preface   i

PART 1: Program Life   1

PART 2: Program Thoughts   35

PART 3: Program Inventories   65

PART 4: Program Notes   103

PART 5: Program Goals and Habits   129

PART 6: Personal Program Observations   159

What's Next?   187

Biography   189

Preface

More GEMS is a second collection of meditations and reflections on alcoholism and recovery.

Like the first volume, this is a dipping book. People dip into it when the mood strikes, take a snippet, think about it, then put the book down till next time.

Some use it as a basis for their morning meditation. Others keep it handy, taking it down once in a while for an occasional browse. I understand many copies reside in bathrooms. (I think a waterproof edition is in order.) Some AA meetings are using *GEMS* as one of their sources of topics for discussion.

I like to think that through these *GEMS*, we are walking together on our journey of happy destiny, trudging into the fourth dimension.

Note on Authorship and Anonymity

In the AA Program, we are publicly anonymous but can be open privately.

If you want to contact me, email me at the address below, and I will strive to get back to you.

andyc@the4thdimension.ca

Proceeds

The writer and publisher hope to engender and enhance spiritual maintenance. Any surplus revenues will be invested in capital and recovery, including Alcoholics Anonymous.

Twelve Steps of Alcoholics Anonymous

Step 1: We admitted we were powerless over alcohol—that our lives had become unmanageable.

Step 2: Came to believe that a Power greater than ourselves could restore us to sanity.

Step 3: Made a decision to turn our will and our lives over to the care of God as we understood Him.

Step 4: Made a searching and fearless moral inventory of ourselves.

Step 5: Admitted to God, to ourselves, and to another human being the exact nature of our wrongs.

Step 6: Were entirely ready to have God remove all these defects of character.

Step 7: Humbly asked Him to remove our shortcomings.

Step 8: Made a list of all persons we had harmed, and became willing to make amends to them all.

Step 9: Made direct amends to such people wherever possible, except when to do so would injure them or others.

Step 10: Continued to take personal inventory and when we were wrong promptly admitted it.

Step 11: Sought through prayer and meditation to improve our conscious contact with God, as we understood Him, praying only for knowledge of His will for us and the power to carry that out.

Step 12: Having had a spiritual awakening as the result of these Steps, we tried to carry this message to alcoholics, and to practice these principles in all our affairs.

PART ONE

Program Life

I n the rooms, we often hear, "Coming to AA gave me two lives."

Our Program is a way to stop drinking and stay stopped. If we practice the Program, the time will come when "we recoil from booze as we would recoil from a hot stove." For alcoholics of our type, this is more than a change of habit; it is a new life, a Program Life, which starts with a sober birth, a first awakening.

Members of AA have a second life. The first life is a drinking life; the second life is a Program Life.

Long-term, contented abstinence from our addiction — our second life — does not happen by accident. We receive this second life through spiritual awakenings. Working the Steps and applying the principles of our Program, we awaken spiritually. Step 12 states that *a* spiritual awakening is *the* specific and unequivocal result of taking the Steps.

The Steps are repeatable. My first sponsor assured me they would not wear out with use, and so far, that has proven true. Every time I have used the Steps in my life, I have had another spiritual awakening. With each awakening, I grow a bit more.

These are meditations and reflections on Program Life — some thoughts and observations on living the Program and building the Program into day-to-day activities, habituating the practice of the Program's "principles in all our affairs."

In the Beginning

At my first AA meeting, I said, "My name is Andy, and I am here." These were the first words in my Program Life.

After the Meeting, an old-timer took me aside and asked, "So what's with, *I am here*?"

I replied, "I think that I have some problems with drinking and sometimes wonder if I should stop, but I am not sure I fit in with this group. I am in third-year law school, with no criminal charges, and doing well. My life is not out of control."

I paused. "But as I said, I am concerned about my drinking."

"Well," he said, "Step One is where we begin. Let's look at it." Pointing to the pull-down shade with the Steps, he said, "Step One has two parts: Powerlessness over alcohol and unmanageability in life. A hyphen separates these two conditions. To qualify for our Program, you only need one."

"It sounds like you think your life is manage-able. That is only one qualification for entry; that leaves powerless over alcohol, the second entrance qualification."

Then he gave me the best news possible, "And for powerlessness over alcohol, we have a test."

I always did well with tests.

The old-timer continued, "Here is the test. For several days, have a couple of drinks, then stop abruptly. If you stay stopped, you will have failed the test; you are not powerless over alcohol. But if you take this test, determined to stop after a couple of drinks, and you cannot stop, and you find you are drunk every time, you pass. You are one of us; you are qualified to come back."

I took the test.

Day one. After a couple of drinks. I said, "Today is not a good day for a test; I'll take the test tomorrow." I drank myself drunk.

Day two. After a couple of drinks, I said to myself, "I missed yesterday's two-drink, then stop test; I should make up the missing day and have four drinks, then stop." I did not stop at four. I drank myself drunk.

On day three, I had two and went home happy and content. In bed, reading in my pyjamas, I thought, "This is great; this is how normal folks drink."

A moment later, after midnight had passed, I thought, "All I need is a nightcap." I passed out at 3 a.m.

I woke up the next morning and had a flash of clarity. For several days, I took the test. I would have a couple of drinks and then drink myself drunk. I could not or would not stop. I was powerless. I had passed the test with a score of 100%.

His wisdom saved my life: that and the hyphen in Step One. I had passed the most crucial test I have ever taken and entered this wonderful AA life.

Doing or Living?

"AA is not something you do; it is a way of life."

In my story, this is a great truth. But this understanding did not arrive like a bolt of lightning; it evolved. Looking back down my road of Happy Destiny, I see there were four phases of AA becoming my way of life.

Phase one: **A place to go**. When I first came to the rooms, AA was a place to go. It was a place where I went to hear about how to stay stopped drinking. I went there to listen to the experts on staying stopped. It was a place to go.

Phase two: **The Fellowship**. After many meetings, I discovered that meetings were more than places to go. There was fellowship. I came to look forward to seeing the guys. I enjoyed the coffee sessions after the meetings, the conversations and humorous bantering. I found Fellowship.

Phase three: **The Program**. By applying the Program's principles to solve problems in life, I learned to apply the Steps in a meaningful and practical manner. I began to practise the principles of the Program in more and more of my affairs. I found the Program.

Phase four: **A way of life**. Phase four was Step 12. I began practising the Program's principles in all my affairs by using the Steps in my daily life. I found a Program Life.

With each phase, I have experienced more happiness, freedom and joy, and at each level, I was convinced it could not get any better. Then it did.

Today, AA is all of these: a place to go, a Fellowship, a Program to follow, and a way of life.

It was, and is, a wonderful "trudge of Happy Destiny."

Spectator Sports

A share from a fellow taking his fifth-year cake at an AA meeting: "For me, drinking was never a spectator sport — ditto my AA Program."

That explained why he had five years. His Program was not a spectator activity; he was on the field and in the game. And I identified with him.

Drinking was not a spectator sport; I never became drunk on another person's drinking; I had to do my own drinking. Neither could I sober up with someone else's Program; I had to do my own Recovery. Nor could I rely on someone else's prayer and meditation practice; I had to do it.

I cannot grow spiritually by watching others any more than I could get the feeling of ease and comfort by watching someone else drink. I must get in the game and on the field. I must play; spectating will not work.

If you are just going to meetings, arriving a bit late and dashing off at the end of the Serenity

Prayer, you are probably spectating, watching the game, not playing the game.

To grow spiritually and have long-term contented sobriety, you must get in the game, commence a prayer and meditation discipline, show up early to meetings, and greet everyone who comes into the rooms.

Cheering in the stands may keep you dry, but for true sobriety, get on the field and into the game.

Life's Paradoxes

According to Webster's Dictionary, Paradox is "A tenet or proposition contrary to received opinion, or seemingly absurd, yet true in fact."

AA Program Life includes paradoxes like, "As we think more *about* ourselves, we think more *of* ourselves." When read quickly, it seems absurd, but on reflection, it makes sense.

AAs spend a lot of time thinking *about* themselves but come to think more *of* themselves.

Sponsors have us go over our drinking history in Step One. We focus on our beliefs in Step Two. We spend time on ourselves when we write out our histories in moral and personal inventories. Then there is Step Five, where I talk about myself.

AAs spend a lot of time thinking about themselves, but in a Program Life, this self-thinking time is structured and purposeful. Structure and purpose that was missing in my former life.

Before I came into the AA rooms, I spent a lot of time thinking about myself, but it was not purposeful or disciplined. My pre-Program habits of self-contemplation were an example of *omphalo-skepsis*, which, according to Webster's Dictionary, means self-absorbed navel-gazing.

This omphaloskeptic path of self-absorbed navel-gazing took me nowhere, or worse, induced brooding, maudlin reflections.

In my Program Life, I spend a lot of time thinking about myself, maybe more than before. Now, however, with the Steps providing structure and purpose for my self-contemplation, different outcomes emerge. The disciplines of inventories, followed by the removal of defects, leads to character development, and character development leads to increased self-respect and self-esteem.

In my Program Life, the paradox, "By thinking more *about* myself, I began to think more *of* myself," is well-founded and true.

Meetings Are Not Sponsors

At a recent AA meeting, a fellow shared, "Meetings are important, but they are no substitute for a sponsor."

He continued, "When I don't have a sponsor, the meeting is my sponsor, and sharing at the meeting becomes a session with my sponsor. Meetings become the time to share the problems of my day and the difficulties of my life. And if I don't have a long list of problems to discuss, I share how things will turn bad in the future. Regardless, it is time to talk about myself."

He continued, "And it's difficult to see how that will benefit anyone. It is all about me and will rarely involve a spiritual solution.

"When I hear people sharing about their problems, I know they don't have a sponsor.

"Sponsors are great for raising and resolving issues. One-on-one with my sponsor, I can discuss problems and develop solutions based on the principles of the Program. Later, I can try the proposed solutions and see how they work.

"When I work with my sponsor and then share at meetings, I share both the problems and the solutions. I share stories about my successes in practising the spiritual principles of the Program in all my affairs."

My friend at the meeting went on, "And even though I have a sponsor, you can spot when I am not calling him. I will share about my day, my crises and my problems — but I will not talk about solutions because the meeting is my sponsor, and I am talking through my problems."

"Now, if you cannot or will not find and use a sponsor, please, please, keep coming to meetings and keep sharing. Tell us how your day has gone. It will keep you from drinking.

"But we will be thinking how much better it would be if you had a sponsor?"

Program Life Is Scientific

Our Program is a spiritual Program, but scientific principles and methods govern our Program Life.

Let me elaborate.

We conduct surveys and inventories of our personal and moral lives. We review our actions and observe and analyze the consequences and the connections between actions and consequences. In this, we are no different from a scientist in a laboratory, studying the results of experiments.

We test ideas and behaviours before we believe them, trying them first to see if they work. We fake it to see if we make it. In this, we are like a scientist testing a theory.

We report and share the results of our experiments. In meetings, we share, "I tried this, it worked," and, "I tried that, and it did not work." We learn by trial and error, both our own experience and the experience of others. Like a scientist, we subject ourselves to peer review.

We must live with an uncompromising acceptance of facts and information, even when we don't like the facts or they don't fit with our theories. Our new way of life demands an open mind and rigorous honesty, the same requirements demanded of a scientist.

If it walks like a duck and quacks, you probably have a duck.

Our Program Life walks and talks like science.

Twelve-Step Workout

An outstanding share at a meeting: "When I was drinking, my spiritual legs atrophied."

He continued, "I was spiritually lazy. So, when confronted with problems, I avoided any solutions that might involve working on my character. I had no spiritual exercise, and my spiritual legs were weakened.

"If circumstances demanded that I do something to deal with a problem, I reached for a bottle. That was my crutch. With my alcoholic crutches, I took weight off my spiritual legs; they did not have to work as hard. As my spiritual legs became weaker from lack of use, alcohol became more than my crutch; it became my wheelchair. Sitting in a spiritual wheelchair, I put no weight on my spiritual legs. With no weight, they became still weaker.

"Eventually," he said, "my spiritual legs could no longer support me. At this point, I fell down and could not get up. I had hit my bottom.

When I stopped drinking alcohol, my spiritual crutches and wheelchair were not available. I had to learn to walk unaided.

"Living without my alcohol support was hard work. My spiritual leg muscles were stiff and sore. I could feel them at the end of the day. But with continuous movement and exercise, they gradually strengthened.

"I started to work the Steps with a sponsor. Now, I had a personal spiritual trainer. The exercise was strenuous, disciplined and purposeful. The muscles of my spiritual legs grew stronger.

"In real life, if I work out in a fitness centre with a personal trainer, my physical legs get stronger. Sober and working the Steps, living a Program Life and working with a sponsor, my spiritual legs get stronger."

He wrapped it up, "So now, I now have a pair of spiritual legs that can carry me around."

Coming and Going

Our Program Life includes sage advice in the form of "sayings."

Some of these aphorisms work both coming and going; you can substitute the critical word in the expression with its opposite, and the phrase still makes sense.

For example, "To think better of yourself, think *more* about yourself." That makes sense. We could also say, "To think better of yourself, think *less* of yourself." That makes sense as well. The expression works — more or less — with either *more* or *less*.

First, "To think better of yourself, think *more* about yourself."

If I follow the Steps, I think a lot about myself, with inventories, Fifth Steps, and defect removals. Working the Steps, I am focused on myself, conducting a disciplined program of change. Following the Steps and living the principles of our Program, I study myself, identify defects, and then remove them with God's help. These were blocking the sunlight of the spirit; with unblocked sunlight of the spirit, I grow to have a greater sense of self-respect and self-love. Thinking *more* about ourselves constructively, as we do in a Program Life, leads us to greater self-esteem, and we come to think *better* of ourselves.

Second, "To think better of yourself, think *less* of yourself."

As I develop spiritually, I find that I think of others first. I spend less time thinking about myself and my agendas. I might be working with a newcomer in the Program or helping a child, spouse, or employer; I start helping those around me and become less self-centred and selfish. I feel the joy of service. This leads to increased self-esteem. Serving others, thinking less of ourselves, we come to think *better* of ourselves.

In our Program Life, with both *more* and *less* time thinking about ourselves, we grow spiritually and think better of ourselves.

Does She Love Me?

If my wife loved me, she would know what to do to make me happy.

And she would have to do it on her own, without any help from me. She'd have to do it on her own because I cannot and will not offer any assistance or guidance as to what would make me happy.

Firstly, I don't know what it might take to make me happy. Secondly, even if I did know, I would not tell her. If I told her what would make me happy, I would have accepted responsibility for my happiness, and I have an allergic reaction to responsibility.

Nonetheless, I demand she make me happy.

Despite the apparent grounds for divorce, I am still married to my wife. Partly because, after adopting a Program Life, I began to relieve her of the task of making me happy.

With discernment granted by my Higher Power, I could see what would make me happy and take responsibility for my happiness. Spiritual growth has meant that I can now understand and be responsible for my happiness.

I wonder what my wife is doing with all the extra time?

Making a Program Sandwich

The Big Book says, "in Step Four, we had to get down to causes and conditions."

Everything happens as a result of causes and conditions.

A fearless and searching moral inventory to identify causes and conditions is an essential part of our Program Life.

Even a peanut butter sandwich has causes and conditions. A peanut butter sandwich is a result of a series of linked causes, a causal chain, in the context of certain necessary conditions.

The causal chain required to make a peanut butter sandwich includes getting the bread from the breadbox, pulling the butter out of the refrigerator and the peanut butter out of the cupboard, then assembling the sandwich.

For the best results, there is a proper sequence for the elements of the causal chain. If you spread the peanut butter without first having a slice of bread, you will have peanut butter all over your hand. It is messy and will not result in a sandwich.

Successful completion of the causal chain requires the necessary conditions. You must have bread in the bread box, peanut butter in the cupboard and you need a knife. With these and other conditions satisfied, the causal chain can be completed, and you can enjoy your sandwich.

To make a peanut butter sandwich, you must complete each of the causes in the chain in the correct order, and all of the conditions must be satisfied.

Step Four is an investigation of negative consequences arising from causes and conditions. The causes and conditions, when identified, can be managed or eliminated, preventing further wrongs and damage.

And our new Program Life is a causal chain, requiring a proper sequence and necessary conditions for optimum outcomes.

Our Program Life includes causal chains like taking personal inventories and identifying and removing defects. There is an optimum sequence for our Program causal chain, the Steps. All of us who have had to make a second amend for our botched first amend can vouch for the need for proper sequencing. Finally, the Program requires certain conditions. Hitting bottom is an essential condition. Coming to believe sound thinking could be restored by a power other than myself was another critical condition. And there are others.

Whether you are making a sandwich preventing future harms or growing in your Program Life, you have causes and conditions.

Paying attention to them through disciplined structured inventories pays dividends.

Stay on the Program Bus

I heard at a recent meeting: "Stay on the Program bus. If you don't like the looks of where you are, and you get off the bus, you might be there for a long time. Stay on the bus, and things will eventually improve."

I have memories from the 60s of being on a Greyhound bus to Winnipeg. Winding its way to the station, the bus went through a rough part of town; it was an undesirable neighbourhood, not an area I would frequent if I had a choice. I remember thinking, "Getting off the bus would not be a good idea."

Eventually, we arrived at the bus depot. It was a nice part of town. There were lovely shops, and the atmosphere was pleasant. I got off the bus and felt safe. It was a place where I could spend some time.

Going through life, the view is sometimes unpleasant. We go through rough patches. Even a Program Life can be difficult, not because of the Program, but because it is life, and life has tribulations and trials.

If I get off my Program bus while going through a rough neighbourhood, I might be stuck in that lousy space for a long time. Staying on the Program bus will eventually bring me to a better place.

If life seems rough, I know from past experiences that things will change. It will eventually improve, but only if I stay on the bus.

Still on the Bus

The last GEM was a metaphor about staying on the Program bus. In this GEM, I will remain on the metaphorical bus.

There are several useful points of comparison between my Program Life and riding in a Greyhound bus.

First, I am not in charge; the driver is in control. I liken the driver to God. When He is in charge, I can sit back and enjoy the ride. And it is best when I am behind the yellow line, well away from the steering wheel.

Second, I can view the world with equanimity, knowing there is a sheet of tempered glass between me and the challenging, cruel world.

Third, there are other passengers. I am not alone; knowing this, I feel serene and calm. In my Program Life, I am not alone. And knowing I am not alone allows me to enjoy the ride with serenity. I feel protected and secure on my Program bus, with sponsors, the Fellowship, and meetings.

Fourth, Greyhound makes sure that passengers arrive at the right station. Greyhound will do whatever it takes to get you where you are supposed to be. It is part of the deal. It is the nature of God to look after His children. On the Program bus, we always arrive where we are supposed to be. It is part of the deal.

In summary, relaxing on the Program bus, I can look out the window, relax with the other passengers and remember that I am under the care and protection of my Higher Power.

No Free Lunch

I was a teenager at an Easter Rally for Christ; I accepted Jesus as my Saviour.

Over the following months, I spoke at rallies, attended Youth for Christ meetings and was generally a young Christian big shot. I had fun, met girls, and the public speaking fed my ego. I was on a frothy spiritual high.

But there was no follow-up, no discipline, no work.

My spiritual high evaporated like a pool of water on hot pavement.

In the Twelve Steps and Twelve Traditions, Bill W. contrasts frothy, effortless, spiritual experiences with the disciplined, action-oriented Twelve Step spiritual awakenings which is our Program life.

On page 32, he states: "…We had been asking something for nothing. The fact was we really hadn't cleaned house so that the grace of God could enter us… In no deep or meaningful sense had we ever taken stock of ourselves…"

He continues: "...Nor [had we] made amends to those we had harmed, or freely given to any other human being without demand for reward. We had not even prayed rightly."

He connects the dots between spiritual growth and work. In so doing, he separates Twelve Step spiritual awakenings in Program Life from frothy emotional religious experiences.

Spiritual growth requires disciplined effort. In our Program Life, we give ourselves to others in service, which engenders spiritual growth. Inventories, amends, and cleaning up the past induce awakenings of the spirit. Making the effort to establish a life of prayer and meditation improves our conscious contact with God.

Work and discipline are our new watchwords.

A spiritual rush, even one as dramatic as Bill's white light experience in Towns Hospital, requires disciplined work to survive, and even more to grow.

We Don't Notice Our Advantages

Hilton Head is a favourite holiday spot for my wife and me. The beaches go for miles along the Atlantic shore. They are broad, progressing from grassy verge to softer sand, then close to the water, where the sand is hard packed. Hard enough to ride a bicycle.

One day I learned a Program Life lesson riding a bicycle on the beach.

With clumsy effort, we pushed our fat-tired beach bikes through the grass, dunes, and soft sand to the hard-packed riding sand near the water. We paused to admire the view and catch our breaths, then mounted our bikes and pushed off.

We gave no thought to which direction we rode. As it happened, it was south.

The ocean was on our left, the dunes on our right. The sun was shining, and the water sparkled; it was a wonderful afternoon.

There was a gentle breeze from the north.

Because we were riding south, we didn't notice the breeze. But noticed or not, it pushed us effortlessly and silently along. We cruised the ocean-side for almost an hour, chatting as we rode along, waving to children, watching birds, and savouring the view. We were happy.

After many miles, we stopped. We turned our bikes around and started back, heading north, into the wind.

We became aware of the soft breeze.

The breeze was not strong, but it was relentless. As the miles grew, I came to resent the wind more and more. I could feel it with every pedal stroke.

The joyful communing with nature was over; I was breathing hard, and there was still a long way to go.

As I laboured into the wind, the asymmetry of my gratitude for the wind at my back going south and my irritation with the same gentle breeze on my nose going north became apparent. I was much more irritated going against the wind than grateful for going with the wind. I felt justified in being irritated because it seemed to me that the effort against the wind was much greater than any benefit with the wind.

Later, exhausted, pushing my bike off the beach at our starting point, I realized I had just experienced a Program Life lesson.

In life, I have headwinds and tailwinds. I thoughtlessly accepted my advantages but deeply resented my disadvantages. When the world unfolds in my favour, I take it and give no thanks but complain and feel bitter resentment when the world is against me.

A good Program friend makes daily gratitude lists. She notes ten things for which she is grateful. She is like a cyclist with a reminder taped to the handlebars, "Remember, you are riding with the wind."

Why bother? There are two reasons: being grateful for the following winds makes the headwinds seem easier, and when troubles come, they seem easier to accept.

When I pay attention to my whole life, I am grateful for tailwinds and come to expect the headwinds.

PART TWO
Program Thoughts

We hear things in our Program that appear simple but are deeply complex.

For example, the word Program. "What is the dictionary meaning of the word *program*?" I looked it up.

Program is a more complicated word than I had thought. It has many dimensions. Program can refer to a planned series of related steps, or a series of instructions.

A program can be a verb or a noun, depending on its context. As a verb, we can program a computer or our life. As a noun, we can execute a program or follow a program; we can work on or from a program.

On the surface, the word is simple, but there is an underlying complexity.

Our 12 Steps and the lessons in our stories are simple. But when we stop to think about them, there are deeper meanings and complexities.

Press the Pause Button

In Step Three, we "turn our will and our lives over to the care of God."

This seems straightforward enough, but how do we do it? For the other Steps there are precise instructions in the Big Book. Step Four has a chart with columns. Steps Six and Seven instructions are detailed: we are directed to take the book down from the shelf and review everything we have done to that point. There is a whole chapter on Step Twelve. But there are no detailed instructions for Step Three in the Big Book.

The detailed instructions for Step Three are in the Twelve and Twelve. In the last paragraph of Chapter Three, Bill finally tells us how to practise Step Three.

There are three parts to the instructions.

The first part is, "In all times of emotional disturbance or indecision, we pause..."

This is critical. When disturbed or deciding something, we hesitate... we pause. And like so many things in our Program, it is not complicated, but it is complex.

With a pause, a moment is taken. That moment allows discernment. We have the time to assess the situation and receive more information. That gives us more material to think about before we act.

And still more is found in the act of pausing.

If we pause before acting, we own the action. Our next act is not the thoughtless reaction of our reptilian brains; it is a considered action. We own it; we are responsible.

The second part is a prayer. Continuing with Bill's instruction, we say, "God grant me the serenity to accept the things I cannot change, courage to change the things I can, and wisdom to know the difference. Thy will, not mine, be done."

In the second part of the instruction, we align our will with His; we turn our minds and hearts towards Him. Oriented thus, things will go better.

Finally, the third part. The third part is hidden in plain sight after the prayer; it is, "Be quiet." Again, referring to Bill's instructions, after the prayer, there is — wait for it — nothing!

After the pause and the prayer, Bill is silent. Silence is the last part of the instruction: Be quiet and listen.

There are three steps to executing the Third Step.

Pause, Pray, then Listen. P.P.L. It is not complicated, but it is complex.

Who Are You Sleeping With?

The topic for the meeting was from the Big Book, "On awakening, let us think about the twenty-four hours ahead. We consider our plans for the day."

A young woman shared, "When I wake up, I review my day with God because I don't sleep with my sponsor."

That struck us as funny. It was funny, and it was wise.

If I have something on my mind or something is coming up, it is always better to talk with my sponsor first. We can sort out flaws and strengths in my thought processes. If I consider an upcoming event or a looming possibility, talking about it releases the anxious energy around what could happen. Either way, I am better prepared.

In addition to helping get my thinking straight and releasing anxious energy, talking with my sponsor gets the problem out of my head. My subjective fears, hopes, and expectations become more objective. Spoken out loud, they are separate from me. They hang like a thought balloon in the space between my sponsor and me. I become calmer; I see the issue more clearly.

When I first wake up, I have the day ahead. Life is about to happen. Many things are on my mind, and many things might come up. If I slept with my sponsor, on awakening, my head still on the pillow, I could talk with him about my upcoming day, and it would go better. But I don't sleep with him; he is not there on my awakening.

Fortunately, when I wake up, God is always there. I can review my day with Him, which then goes better.

When I tell God about all the meetings and phone calls I see coming up, I am prepared for both the difficulties and opportunities I can see. I am also better prepared for the eventualities I do not see.

Talking with God, I get the problem out of my head. I perceive that which had been in my mind with greater objectivity. I see possibilities more clearly. I see problems from more than one side, and that saves emotional energy. The day goes better.

I don't sleep with my sponsor, but I can review my day with God on awakening. He is always there.

What We Know that Just Ain't So

"What gets us into trouble is not what we don't know. It's what we know for sure that just ain't so." This is wisdom from Mark Twain.

When I get into trouble and look back, I see that what I thought I knew was just not so. These mistaken preconceptions filtered my view of reality; they created a distortion field, and that distortion field got me in trouble.

The distortion field is most dangerous when "what I think I know" about myself "just ain't so."

What I know about myself is often wrong, and my false ideas about myself get me into trouble. It got me in trouble when I was drinking and continues to get me in trouble in sobriety.

By working the Program, I can see myself more clearly and remove the distortion field created by "what I know to be true about myself, that just ain't so."

When I use the Steps of the Program, what I think I know about myself that just ain't so is replaced by the truth about myself.

The truth is revealed in taking pen in hand and writing out my inventories. I cannot BS the paper; I am confronted with reality and cannot hide behind the distortion field of what I know that just ain't so. With a good Step Four and Five, I clearly see myself, and this is repeated in Step Ten.

Inventories start the removal of the distortion field, and making amends finishes the job. When I make amends, I perceive the reality of my character more comprehensively. The truth about myself and what I have done is in my face. Sitting down with the person to whom I am making the amend, the reality of my defective character sits across from me.

Living a Program Life removes "what I know that just ain't so," and the troubles I get into.

Causes, Condition, and Conditions

In Step Four, we "get down to causes and conditions."

Having a dictionary handy when thinking about the Program is always a good idea. Looking up the official meaning of words, we find insights that otherwise escaped us.

Taking my own advice, I looked up the meaning of *causes* and *conditions*.

Causes: no surprises there. In the dictionary, a cause is a cause, "something that brought another thing into being."

But the word *conditions*? Wow, big surprise. *Condition* is a complicated word. For example, there is a difference between *condition* and *conditions*, the singular and plural. The plural of a word usually means multiples of the singular. Think of dog and dogs, cat and cats... cause and causes. But not so with *condition* and *conditions*.

A dictionary meaning of *condition* pertains to the inside of an object: "The working order of the thing." When I ask the question, "What is my condition?" I am asking, "What is my working order? What is going on inside?"

But the meaning of *conditions* refers to the state of things outside the object. When I ask, "What are my conditions," I am asking, "What are my circumstances? What is going on around me?"

To get down to causes, condition, and conditions, we need to inventory all three elements and synthesize how the three work together. Causes: the trigger. Condition: our insides, our perceptions and attitudes, together with our allergic reaction to alcohol. And conditions: our environment.

Then we can analyze how they all work together, like this:

A cause: We want a drink, which we know will make us feel better.

Two internal conditions: We have a physical allergy to alcohol. And a mental quirk that allows us to believe drinking will not cause a problem this time.

And one external condition: Booze is available.

All three work together for another drunken spree.

Eliminate any one of the three, and I stay sober. My allergic reaction to grain alcohol is permanent. And there will always be liquor around.

Therefore, if I find I want a drink, I can still have the physical allergy, and booze may be available; but if I remove the mental quirk and remember past drunks with sufficient force, I remain sober.

Dictionaries are handy; they lead to insights.

Test and Verify

Our Program Life includes self-observations.

For many years, in my inventories, I studied my reactions to the world. This revealed much, but I wondered about a more active process of self-discovery. I decided I could take a different, more scientific approach — to test and verify rather than react and record. After all, my sponsor preached the virtues of action before belief. "Fake it till you make it" was his favourite expression.

For my first proactive experiment, I decided to test a new approach to my morning commute, to use my drive to work as my laboratory for a new way of acting.

For one week, I tried attitude 'A.' As soon as I started the car, I began looking for an opportunity to let someone in front of me, allow someone room to enter traffic, or allow someone to get where they needed to be.

All other variables were held constant; I was in the same car and took the same route, surrounded by the same bad drivers who were out to get me. The construction crews and blockages were unchanged.

I measured my sense of well-being at the end of the commute. I used a scale of 1 to 10. If I was relaxed and feeling good about life, the score was 10; if I was agitated and worried about the day, my score was 1. My average score at the end of the commute for the week was 6.0. Not once was I angry or upset.

At noon, I was even more serene than at the end of my commute. I scored myself again, and my average daily score had increased to 8.0. Attitude 'A' set an upward trend that had a lasting effect on my day.

The following week, I left my garage with attitude 'B.' With grim determination to get to the office as quickly as possible, no matter what, I would drive as if I owned the road. Again, all other variables were held constant. I was in the same car and drove the same route, but there was a new score. My score on arrival was 3.0. Every day I was irritated and upset by the drivers around me, and the construction delays had me pounding on the steering wheel.

And the attitude of my drive had a lasting impact on my day. My noon scores were an average of 2.0. By noon I was tenser and more worried than when I had arrived at the office. The lousy start with attitude 'B' set a downward trend in motion that continued throughout the day.

Attitude 'A' clearly worked. *Test and verify:* Those were the new watchwords of my Program Life.

Humility is Demanding

My Uncle, Bill C., was a lion in the Program. We often talked about the Program. One day, I asked how he defined *humility*.

He said, "Humility means an accurate and true understanding of myself and my situation."

I was surprised. Then I wondered, *Why am I startled?* What did the word humility mean to me?

I thought, to demonstrate humility, I would say, I am a nothing, a nobody, a shameful man who counts for nothing. I have little worth and many defects.

My first thought about humility was "self-effacement and self-denigration."

But this would be dangerous and false humility. Not only would it allow me to wallow in self-pity, but it could also allow me to evade the responsibilities that come with my station in life. Having no responsibilities, I could be childish and grandiose, gossip and whine, a poor example of long-term sobriety at home, in the office, or at AA meetings.

The truth is, I am a lawyer, with some prominence in the community; I am a father and husband; I am a long-time AA member. I help newcomers; people at meetings pay attention to what I share. I have defects, but fewer than before. I am striving to maintain a fit spiritual condition.

That is a more truthful and accurate summary of myself and my situation than self-absorbed abnegation. And it confronts me with duties and obligations.

As a father and husband, I must take care and practise patience and love at home. As a community leader, I must be careful with what I say and do.

I must honour my role as a long-time AA member, strive to be attractive, and offer something that someone might want.

False humility is lazy and allows me to avoid responsibilities, to behave in a childish, self-centred manner. True humility is demanding. With true humility, I am accountable and responsible.

Uncle Bill had a good point.

Skiing to the
Fourth Dimension

In my youth, I taught skiing; it was my first career.

I learned to diagnose skiing problems presented by my students. One technique, study the tracks of the skis left in the snow.

Imagine a ski hill. I am standing beside you. It is a private lesson. Explaining the process, I say, "I will go first and make several turns. After I stop, I will call for you to come down. Turn where I turn. I will set a track that you can follow. I want to study a series of your turns carefully, to see what is going on."

I push off and take a series of turns on the freshly groomed snow. I stop, turn, and look up to you and say, "Your turn; follow my tracks."

I watch you carefully, five complete turns. You followed my track and turned where I had turned — but there is a problem. With each turn, you are more out of balance. In the end, the last turn, you are discombobulated; arms flailing, you come to an ungraceful stop, panting with exertion.

Puzzled, I can't see what caused the problem.

"Wait here," I say.

Leaving you to catch your breath, I climb back up the hill, studying the track left in the snow. The imprint your skis leave in the snow shows more than you can imagine. For each turn, the track shows where your weight was focused on your skis as you turned; I can see where you set your edges, where you started the slide portion of the turn, how your weight moved during the turn. The track in the snow is the history of each turn.

And there it is — the problem, written in the snow. Though the problem showed up in the last turns, it began in the first turn and grew with each succeeding turn.

The edge set of the skis left in the snow shows that your weight was on the back of your skis as you started the first turn. You were on your heels from the beginning. I did not see it as you were skiing, but there it was, in the snow track.

With each turn, the problem magnified. You shifted more weight to the back of your skis in each of the second and third turns; by the fourth, you were on your heels. No wonder you had to muscle through the last turn, unbalanced and uncomfortable.

Doing a written inventory, we can see our day like we can see our tracks in the snow.

At the end of a hard day — harsh words, angry, and impatient. We can see where we came to a stop, off-balance and arms flailing.

But as in skiing, we have to identify where the problem started. Where did things begin to go wrong? Where did the self-centred attitudes commence?

The problem may have started at breakfast. We became upset because our toast was burnt, our eggs were runny, whatever. We were on our back foot, and it went downhill from there. By the end of the day, we are on our heels, emotional arms flailing.

It is hard work, reading ski tracks or seeing our inventory clearly. The first time we do it, we don't see it very clearly; it takes practice. It helps to have an instructor, or a sponsor, to show us the error in our tracks.

Then, with time and practice, we catch ourselves at the commencement of the problems rather than the end.

And now, you can see why, when you call your sponsor about a temper tantrum at home, he asks for a review of the entire day. He wants to study your tracks.

Unwinding Your History

Heard at a meeting: "With inventories, we unwind our histories."

I remember my grandmother had a ball of string in a kitchen drawer. Whenever she had a piece of string from a package, she would save it. She would reach into the drawer, take out her ball, and wrap the new bit of string around it. It started small, but after many years, it was about the size of a softball — a pretty, multi-coloured softball.

When she needed a bit of twine, she reached for the ball — unwinding the string and laying each piece on the table until she found the piece she needed.

I can see my history as my grandmother's ball of string and my inventories as that unwinding process.

My life was different bits of string wrapped up in a solid ball. As I wrote my inventory, I unwound the bits and laid them out on the table. Some bits are long; some are short. There were bits of rough brown twine and smooth white thread, a red string, and a green string.

Doing an inventory unwinds my life, like unwinding my grandmother's twine ball. The various bits of string represent different elements of my story. There are different colours for happy and sad times. Different lengths for long and short relationships. Different types for various activities, rough brown twine for work and smooth white thread for AA meetings.

When I held my grandmother's ball of string, I could only see the top layers. The inner layers were hidden, but as I unwound the string, inner layers were revealed.

In my inventories, I unwind the ball. Writing out the stories, I am pulling bits of string from the ball of twine. Separating and laying out the bits of yarn on the table, I can see them - different colours, lengths, and textures.

In my inventories, using pen and paper, I can see the colour, length, and texture of the parts of my life. And with each inventory, I unwind more of my life's stories. Seeing the words written on the paper allows me to look at each bit of my life. Just as there are different colours and types of twine to unwind, there are different lessons to learn and defects to remove.

With inventories, I unwind my life.

Membership Priceless

Years ago, Mastercard had a series of television commercials with a common theme. Each commercial reviewed the elements of a vignette the viewer could recognize. It might be an event or an activity. The background announcer read out the price of each part of the event or activity in the ad, with a closing line, summarizing the purchases — as "priceless."

I remember one. Two people were in love, walking along a downtown sidewalk. The voice-over said, "Supper, $150; flowers, $35; a great movie, $32," then closed with the summation, "Great memories with someone special... priceless."

There was a message in the advertisement. Each part had a price that you could total in your mind as the announcer read them out. But the total event, the result, did not have a price. It had great value, but no price. It was priceless.

An alcoholic life is much like that.

I can imagine a Mastercard commercial for AA newcomers.

The scene opens in a church basement. The usual AA materials are on the walls. Coffee pot and literature on the table. The camera zooms in on one unhappy individual sitting at the back; he is miserable and hungover from his last drunk. The deep-voiced announcer intones a narrative: "A DUI, $15,000; a divorce, $30,000; loss of employment, $50,000." Then, a dramatic pause followed by, "Membership in AA... priceless."

Each element of our path to the Program has a price. We can see it and total the dollars it cost.

But membership in AA, priceless.

Letting Go

The subject of the meeting was the Serenity Prayer. A young lady shared, "Forgiveness is letting go of what I think it should be…Thanks, I pass." That was all she wanted to say.

I was puzzled by the share. Over breakfast the next morning, I recalled the share and understood what she was saying: Letting go of what I think things should be, is the Serenity Prayer, and it is an act of forgiving.

With wisdom, provided by God, I can discern that which I cannot change. Then with serenity provided by God, I can accept that reality.

Forgiveness is not about who harmed whom more; forgiveness is not about forgetting; forgiveness is not about ignoring the hurt.

Forgiveness is accepting reality that I cannot change, which is the heart of the Serenity Prayer.

Asymmetrical Forgiveness

For me, forgiveness is a necessary part of Step Eight, the precursor to making amends in Step Nine. I must forgive the people I have harmed before making an amend.

This is obvious if the person committed great harm to me. Before I can make an amend, I must forgive the harm done to me. Only then can I communicate effectively. If I have not forgiven them, the damage done to me remains in my mind as I try to make the amend, and garbles the message.

But oddly, this is true for the obverse, when my part is large, when I have caused more harm than I received. When I am clearly in the wrong, I must first forgive the other side. If I don't, the comparatively small offence they created is on my mind and this impedes our communication. Eliminating it by forgiving allows the communication to flow without turbulence.

Let me share a personal story.

My wife looks after all our paperwork. She deals with all the filing, reporting, management, and letter writing for our personal and business affairs.

Once in a blue moon, she will ask me to sign something.

As she knows, I am not a morning person. One day, before I had finished my breakfast, she asked me to sign a document. Irritated by the interruption, I signed the papers with a snappish tone and dramatic heaving sighs.

Boy, was I ever in the wrong. She had merely interrupted my breakfast to complete a task for my benefit, and I displayed childish petulance—score 2 units of harm for her, versus 100 units of hurt for me.

I realized that I had to make an amend for my offensive and childish behaviour.

An intuitive thought occurred, "First, I have to forgive her for interrupting my breakfast routine."

Then the rational thought occurred, "I was way more in the wrong; she will have to forgive me. I don't have to forgive her; it would be arrogant and inappropriate for me to forgive her. I am the offender, not her. It was all my fault."

The intuitive thought prevailed over the rational, and I said prayerfully, "I forgive my wife for interrupting my breakfast to sign the paperwork that she had carefully prepared."

I forgave her for the trivial offence of interrupting my breakfast, then went to make an amend.

Walking over to her office, I gently knocked, entered, and said, "I am deeply sorry that I snapped at you this morning. I hope that you can forgive me and accept this sincere apology."

Because of my prior forgiveness of her minor harm, my entire tone, posture, and attitude were right. There was no tension in my voice, no reservation in my language. The communication was clear and there was no turbulence.

Because of this, and her loving and kind nature, she said, "No, I was wrong to bother you; I know how much your quiet time means in the morning. I was inconsiderate. I hope that you can forgive me. Come, let me kiss you to makeup."

Not only was the amend more effective, *but she was apologizing to me*. Boy, this program works!

Humility Is Active

We usually use the words *humility* or *humble* as something passive.

Humility is a word that does not reflect action or movement. Humble stands still, in contrast to words like *go*, *act*, or *move*. We usually imagine a humble person as quiet, self-effacing, and meek, standing silent at the back of the room.

We rarely associate the idea of moving with humility; "humble" and "charging ahead" are not found together in the same sentence. I doubt you have ever heard anyone say, "As he surged forward, you could see his humility."

However, for Bill W., humility is an active word, humility is action. It is working, doing and moving in "obedience to God and His will for us."

It is not static or passive; it is not standing head hung low in self-effacing abjuration. It is action, marching forward, head high, following God's will and direction.

Go humble, Go!

PART THREE

Program Inventories

Through moral and personal inventories we identify defects and assets.

Over the years, I have observed the diminution and disappearance of defects and the enhancement of assets.

Both defects and assets are important, but we tend to focus more on the defects than the assets. The emphasis on defects makes sense. Removal of defects has a double effect. First, removal of a defect brings serenity and calm. Second, removal of a defect allows assets to grow. For this reason, an emphasis on the liability side is appropriate.

But we cannot forget assets. It is essential to include assets. Track your progress with asset development to understand and appreciate growth. It is a powerful incentive to progress spiritually.

We each find our own balance.

Spotlights and Shadows

The inventory process is a spotlight, illuminating problems that stand out like towers and poles on the landscape of our character. With the bright illumination, we can see the shadows created by these defects, the harms and the damage.

The character defects and the harms they created are easy to see in early sobriety. They are obvious: repaying money, making apologies for destructive behaviours, and rectifying wrongs.

With the passing of sober time, doing many inventories, and making amends, the nature of the defects revealed in personal inventories seems different.

In my story, older defects were large and plain; newer defects were subtle. They shape-shifted like Windigo, the Ojibway spirit who appears in different animal forms and can change his shape at will. Like this ancient spirit, my defects were destructive behaviours covered up by dishonest and self-seeking

motives, masked by cloaks of self-justification—
a hundred forms of fear, subtle and disguised.

Fortunately, with many inventories under my
belt, I could discern the nature of new defects, and
with God's help, attack and remove them.

And, with each removal, my assets flourished.

Are You Regular?

In the Big Book of Alcoholics Anonymous, Bill Wilson recites a business truth: "A business that does not do a regular inventory usually goes broke."

Well-run businesses have a yearly inventory cycle: An annual inventory to support year-end financial statements, which are reviewed by an auditor and reported to the shareholders; quarterly inventories for statements presented to the Board; and weekly inventory reports to allow management to track performance.

I have found it helpful to follow the annual cycle that a well-run business would follow. I do a yearly inventory to prepare for a year-end review with my external auditor, my spiritual coach, and report to God, quarterly internal reviews with my responses to see how I am doing; and weekly summaries to know if I am on the beam.

With this inventory rhythm, I lower the risk of spiritual insolvency.

Well-run businesses work, with discipline and structure, to find and face facts about themselves and their operations. They go to this effort to see problems early before they grow too large to handle. The inventories not only point to problems, they illuminate solutions.

If businesses don't follow these disciplines, then as Bill warns, they usually go financially broke.

If AAs don't have regular inventory habits to find and face facts about themselves, they usually go spiritually broke.

I know this from experience; I have become nearly bankrupt spiritually because I did not do regular inventories.

Avoiding finding and facing the facts about myself, problems piled up, and I almost went bust.

After several close brushes with spiritual bankruptcy, I have learned that continuous fact-finding and fact-facing, through regular structured and disciplined inventories, are essential to maintain my spiritual life.

Moral Versus Personal

Bill W. uses two adjectives to describe Program inventories: *moral* and *personal*. Step Four is a *moral* inventory. Step Ten is a *personal* inventory.

Now, I don't want to make too much of the distinction between moral and personal. A careful reading of the Big Book and The Twelve by Twelve shows that Bill Wilson used the words interchangeably.

But we should not ignore the distinction either.

My experience suggests there is a difference between the "moral" in Step Four and the "personal" in Step Ten.

My early Step Four inventories were moral. Questions of right and wrong, harms and damages. Where had I been wrong? Where had I harmed someone? Where had I done something requiring restitution?

Later, with Step Ten inventories, I moved from *moral* to *personal*. Personal inventories included moral and more.

Here is my story.

I start an entire inventory process every year on my AA birthday.

I follow the classic four-column inventory instructions found in the Big Book. Those instructions start with Column 1, which Bill describes as "a grudge list."

My early Step Four grudge lists were names of people I had wronged or harmed and situations requiring restitution. One year, my grudge list changed; I transitioned from Step Four inventories to what I now regard as my annual Step Ten inventory.

That year, I went back and re-read the instructions in the Big Book. I realized Bill's grudge list was not a list of people I had harmed. The grudge list was a list of people who made me "angry" or "burned me up," regardless of whether or not I was aware of some harm or wrong I had done to them. Focusing on what made me angry rather than who I harmed, I found myself developing a more extensive grudge list.

I still listed situations and relationships where I had wronged or harmed, but I was also listing relationships that made me feel bad, relationships that were off-putting or left a bad taste, relationships that were "just not right."

The grudge list had become personal as well as moral.

This new approach to my annual grudge list expanded the scope of my search for defects of character. I am finding more and more about myself and my personality and improving all my relationships.

Inventory of Principles

In my many inventories, I had listed people and institutions. Names of people, too many to be listed here, and many institutions; the tax department, the RCMP, churches, and other institutions come to mind.

But Bill listed three categories: people and institutions, and a third, principles.

One year, in my annual inventory, I noticed the third category. I stopped short and thought, "I have never dealt with principles in an inventory."

I was puzzled. How do you name a principle? What harm could I cause a principle? How do I resent a principle?

Re-reading the instructions in the Big Book for the names on a "grudge list," I noticed the sentence, "We listed people, institutions or *principles* with whom we were angry... So we were sore. We were burned up."

I thought for a moment. What principles make me "angry," "sore," or "burned up"?

A conversation with a sponsor came to mind. I had called him to whine about an investment that was going bad. He said, "You always get upset when you lose money."

He was right. Losing money burns me up, makes me sore, and makes me angry. I realized I had my first principle, "I don't like the principle — I can lose money."

I had my first principle for my grudge list.

Then, quick as a flash, another principle came to mind, "I don't like it that God seems to hide. He should be out in the open."

The mental floodgates opened. I don't like that I have to work hard to make money. I don't like that people get sick. I don't like to pay taxes. On and on I went. I did not like this; I did not like that.

There were many principles I did not like; they made me angry and burned me up.

I added these principles to my grudge list and worked through the second and third columns of the inventory, "What happened?" and "How did it affect me?" The answers for various principles all had the same theme: *The principle operated, the world unfolded, I did not like the results, and I became angry.*

Column 4, "What Was My Part?" Those also had the same theme: I had no part in the creation of the principles. They are universal laws. My part was not adjusting to the requirements of reality. I did not accept these realities; I resented them. I then nurtured and fed those resentments.

Including principles in my inventory revealed the exact nature of a character defect. I did not want to bend myself to the principles of reality. The inventory showed the exact nature of my shortcomings. And it pointed to the solution: acceptance.

Adding principles to my inventories took a long time, but it was worth it when the penny dropped. I saw both the problem and the solution.

False Flags

Ships fly the flag of their country of origin. In nautical jargon, they are flying their true colours. If they want to hide their true country of origin, they fly a false flag, the flag of another country. The nationality of the vessel is misrepresented.

We often fly false flags for the world to see. We fly flags that misrepresent our character to an observer. In doing this, we deceive others, and if we fly them long enough, we deceive ourselves.

Years ago, I was a young lawyer building a practice. I worked hard and long hours. My beloved wife managed the home front and looked after our two boys, leaving me to "bring home the bacon." I was aware of the small amount of time I spent with my two young children. It bothered me, but work trumped family at that stage of my life.

One day, I was lunching with some friends. They were, like me, young lawyers and young fathers. We were going on about the joy we experienced with our children. We waxed poetic about the joys of fatherhood.

As we talked, I noticed we only spoke in generalities, never specific events or stories. I thought to myself, "I know these guys. They work as long and hard as I do. They don't spend any more time with their children than I do."

I said nothing but noted that my platitudes about the joys of fatherhood misrepresented the amount of actual time with my children. And misstated my priorities; I was flying a false flag.

I often fib about what I am doing. My talk does not reflect my walk. I might forgive myself and say that these differences are aspirational, that I am speaking how I wish one day to live, but in truth, I hide my behaviours with the right words. I fly false flags.

Regular inventories reveal my false flags. We do inventories and subject our lives to rigorous and honest appraisals. We talk with sponsors about what we are doing and what we are saying. We find and face our hard objective facts.

And in so doing, we find our authentic selves and fly our true colours.

Let the Healing Begin

For my annual inventory I follow the classic Big Book four-column format. I write a "grudge list," a list of names; I write names, nothing more.

I don't think. If a name comes to mind, it goes on the list. I let my mind flow through my pen in a stream of consciousness. The names tumble out of my head onto the paper.

Later I will get to "What Happened?" and why the names are on my grudge list. First, I get the names on the paper.

I restrict myself to writing names for a reason. In my experience, writing a grudge list is more than gathering names. By writing the names on the list, I subconsciously start the remedial processes of making things right.

When I write the name, the person, institution, or principle, it is outside of my head; when it is on the paper or the computer screen, I can no longer deny the problem. It is there on the paper. There is something magical about seeing the name written down and acknowledging that the name has been on my mind.

If the name is echoing around in my mind, emotions like envy, fear, hate, etc., are generated and amplified, but when I write the name and see it, the emotional echo in my head stops. By writing the words, I begin to think objectively about the person, principle, or institution.

I could say that it "objectifies" the person, principle, or institution, and that would be a truth, but it would not be a complete truth. There is another dimension to the phenomenon.

It may seem counter-intuitive, but a greater sense of empathy comes with increased objectivity.

When I see the name on the paper. the emotions I feel with the name echoing inside my head become calm. In this calm, my thoughts expand, which creates a capacity to see what the person might see and feel. A greater sense of empathy emerges in this expanded space.

The impact of writing the name and seeing it outside my head is powerful and begins the process of resolving the issues surrounding the person, principle, or institution.

Writing the name begins the healing.

Special Names

In inventories, some names are special. Here is a story of how we can powerfully investigate a special relationship.

Years ago, I was working with a fellow who was having trouble with his wife, or she with him. Regardless, the marriage was troubled.

I suggested he do an inventory of the relationship.

We agreed on the classic four-column method of inventory laid out in the Big Book, but we added a twist.

Usually, in Column 1, we list names of people who burn us up and make us angry, but this grudge list would have only one name — Phyllis, his wife. So we decided his wife, that one name, represented many roles; each role could be a different name.

Here is the column list that we developed (first three columns only.)

Role	What Happened?	How Did It Affect Me?
Phyllis — lover	Things were excellent here, no problems.	I feel fine.
Phyllis — business partner (They owned property together.)	She was spending way too much money. This was the subject of many arguments.	Ouch, fear and anxiety about our future.
Phyllis — mother of the three children	She was good with the children.	I feel good about this aspect of our marriage.
Phyllis — social companion (How does he feel about walking into a party with her on his arm?)	She has a loud, braying laugh and makes poor jokes. I repeatedly apologized for her behaviours.	I feel shame and wish that I were somewhere else.

Role	What Happened?	How Did It Affect Me?
Phyllis — a travel companion (Does he enjoy spending holidays with her?)	She is demanding when on holidays, always bitching.	I dread going away with her, and I cannot seem to do enough for her.
Phyllis — a friend (Is she a friend?)	Yes. She is a good friend.	I am passing the driveway test. When I come home after a long day and see her car in the driveway, my heart lifts with joy, I am looking forward to seeing her.

Each name/role was a different aspect of a complex relationship. Each name/role yielded a different answer for Column 2, "What Happened?"

The lover, mother and friend parts were excellent, but finance and travel companion — these were problematic. With this powerful inventory tool, he could see what areas of the relationship were working and which were not.

Column 3, "How Did It Affect Me?" yielded even more food for thought.

The discoveries continued in Column 4, "What Was My Part" were revealing. In each area, he could see his part more clearly. Sometimes it was his anger or fear, or he was utterly self-absorbed. He could acknowledge his fear and sullen, resentful reactions to her behaviours and actions; he could see his lack of courage to ask for a change and the lack of serenity to accept her behaviours.

And this inventory process also showed where he was not at fault.

With these insights, he could focus on areas in which he had a part. And he could see areas to be grateful.

We had developed a powerful inventory tool.

Just the Facts

I have finished my grudge list. Now I consider Column 2 — "What Happened?" Why are those names on my grudge list?

Column 2 of a four-column inventory is the "What Happened" column. When I start this column, I am reminded of Sgt. Joe Friday of the 1950s TV show *Dragnet*.

When he interviewed someone, he would say, "Just the facts ma'am, just the facts."

In Column 2, we list the facts. Just the facts, nothing more. The facts are usually something the person named in column #1 did or something that happened because of them.

But facts and feelings can be confused. I worked with a sponsee years ago; his Column 2 had entries like "He made me angry," "It upset me," and "She made me feel ashamed."

I read these entries, turned to him, and asked, "Do you realize that you have written down feelings, not facts?"

Not missing a beat, he said, "Well, those are the facts; the facts of how I felt."

He had me, but only for a second. I asked, "If I was looking at the situation, would I see your feelings? Let us consider facts to be things that an outside viewer would see. A third party cannot see your feelings."

Why stick to facts and ignore feelings? In my experience, writing about my feelings in Column 2 clouds the perceptions of what happened. Sticking to the observable facts clearly reveals what happened; clarity that is lost when I include feelings.

For example, in statements like, "He made me angry because he disagreed with me," or "I became upset when he refused to see things my way," the emotional baggage of the "anger" or "upset" emotion dilutes the self-absorbed triviality of the facts that gave rise to the resentment.

Standing bare, without the emotions, I can see the self-absorbed triviality of, "He disagreed with me," or "He refused to see things my way."

Including the feelings masked the trivial and self-centred quality of my resentful reaction.

Sticking to "just the facts" allows the truth of the situation to emerge, in all its embarrassing glory.

A good reason to remember Sgt. Joe Friday, "Just the facts, ma'am, just the facts."

Revealing the Feelings

I wrote the names in Column 1, my grudge list. Then, in Column 2, I wrote the facts — why each name is on the list. Now, I use the same free-flow brain dump to describe how I was affected.

A free-flow brain dump allows my deepest thoughts to emerge.

If I stop to think, my mind steps between my thoughts and the paper. It interrupts the flow. It translates, interprets, and justifies my thoughts.

Thinking dresses up the thoughts; if the flow is free and unthinking, the thoughts are naked. And in their nakedness, I see repeated patterns of words and phrases. The flow of thoughts displays my sub-conscious attitudes and perceptions.

Let me share with you how it has worked for me.

When I start Column 3, jotting down words that describe how the names and facts in Columns 1 and 2 affected me, there are no surprises for the first few names. After a few entries, though, I begin to see repeated words and phrases, and these newly revealed patterns are always surprising.

I still remember the shock the first time I had this experience.

I was young in the program, and it was an early inventory. Twenty minutes of free-flow writing every day. With no thought, I just wrote what came to mind.

One day, I wrote a phrase. It described a reaction to a girl. It was a girl I had known as a young teen. It came to mind, and I wrote it down before I thought about it.

I stopped and mentally rejected the idea because it expressed a rude sentiment, a belief that I would have found offensive if I saw it in someone else. I certainly did not think that it was a sentiment that I possessed.

As I started to cross it out with my pen, I thought, "You have written this phrase before." I looked back over the previous pages of entries. Sure enough, a couple of days before, I had used the exact phrase regarding another girl. On further investigation, I saw I had written the same thing, almost word for word, no less than four times with four different girls. Ouch! I did not want to believe that I had this attitude towards women. But there it was, on the paper.

If I had stopped to think, my conscious mind would have stopped me from writing that phrase. With a free flow, it was allowed to manifest.

I closed the notebook, sensing that I had uncovered a vital pattern. I saw the exact nature of a defect that needed attention. I talked with my spiritual coach. I asked God to help me with it, and He did in His good time.

My story of identification, clarification, and God's victory over that problem is now part of my story, shared with many sponsees.

What Was My Role?

In Column 3, I answered the question, *How was I affected by the facts I had listed?* And in the free flow of writing, I saw patterns of thought and attitudes.

And patterns of thought and attitude emerge in the free flow of writing in Column 4, when I answer the question, "What Was My Part?"

I cannot BS the paper; the patterns and defects are explicit. And because they are on paper, I cannot deny the words and phrases that bubble up from my subconscious.

I don't see any patterns for the first few names. But, working down the list and describing my role or my part, patterns of words appear.

As I work down the grudge list of names, facts, and reactions, identifying "my role," repeated words and phrases begin to emerge. Phrases such as, "I was rude," "I talked behind her back," "I had made a joke at his expense," or other phrases, like "I treated them with prideful arrogance," and "I refused to forgive them," show up again and again.

The first time I did my inventory on an Excel spreadsheet, technology revealed the patterns. As I typed the words that came to mind into the Column 4 cells, the spreadsheet's autofill function prompted words I had previously typed in other cells. For example, I would type, "I refused…" and the spreadsheet auto-fill would leap up with, "I refused to forgive them." The autofill function on my computer confronted me with the repetitive reality of what was bubbling up from my subconscious.

As in Column 3, Column 4 of the inventory process reveals hidden patterns. In Column 3, attitudes and perceptions; in Column 4, more profound spiritual defects that needed removing.

Looking back, I can see that sometimes things were hidden because of denial; at other times, delusion; and still other times, ignorance.

Either way, I would say on completion, "Wow, I did not see that coming."

The Confessional
Conversation

The inventory is now complete. While it is still fresh in my mind, I book time with my spiritual coach, Father Kevin. We have been working together for over 30 years.

When we meet, we have our annual Step Five interview. Over the years, our Step Five process has evolved to become both a confession and a conversation.

Firstly, It is a confession that releases the internal tensions created by hidden secrets.

Those of us who have done a thorough Step Five know the relief that comes with confession.

But there is more than confession. Father Kevin and I have a conversation. We talk about the stories and patterns. We look for the words that best describe the exact nature of the character defects.

I need to admit to God, Kevin, and myself the "exact nature of the wrongs." To admit something, I need to speak it, and to speak it, I need the words. The words to articulate the "exact nature of the wrongs" emerge in the back and forth of conversation.

For example, one year, my inventory included many stories of my fear of "looking less than."

But what was the exact nature of the wrong? At first, we talked about the fear of being less than perfect. Was my fear of "looking less than" a fear of not being perfect? That did not seem quite right. We talked then about pride and ego and wondered if this fear of "looking less-than" was another manifestation of ego and self-centeredness. That was close, but it did not seem complete. As the conversation continued, Kevin asked, "On whom do you depend for your self-worth?"

That was it.

My fear of "looking less than" was a dependency on what I thought others thought of me. In the conversation, we had teased out the exact nature of the problem, the underlying theme of the defect.

This is the second part of the Fifth Step confessional conversation. The confession releases the energy created by the secrets, and the conversation names the defect's exact nature.

That is my experience and joy.

Navel-Gazing

This GEM is for the word geeks.

Some words are fascinating. The other morning, I received a new word from my word-a-day app. It was the best new word I have had for years.

"Omphaloskepsis"

Pronunciation: (om-fuh-lo-SKEP-sis) Meaning:

1. Contemplation of one's navel.

2. Complacent and self-indulgent introspection. Etymology: From Greek omphalos (navel) + skepsis (the act of looking, examination).

I shared this definition with my wife, who is familiar with my Program. She laughed out loud and said, "That would be a handy word to have in AA."

I thought she was laughing at my AA friends and their self-obsessed habits. I believe, in retrospect, that she was laughing at me, because I tend toward omphaloskepsis.

I often think about myself, and without the Program, my self-thoughts are omphaloskeptic — self-absorbed and self-indulgent navel-gazing. But with the Program, my "self" thoughts are along the lines of "To thine own self be true," not "To thine own self be indulgent."

Let me elaborate.

Without the Program, my "self" thoughts are damaging. I think about my little emotions. I obsess over minor slights. I am preoccupied with how I look. This is more complicated than you might think. I have a first-order worry — what you think about me — and I have a second-order worry — what *I* think you think about me.

But, with the structure and discipline of the Program, I properly think about myself. I can live the AA motto, "To thine own self be true." Life is no longer all about me. I stop fussing over your facial expressions and verbal asides, imagining you are always thinking about me.

When practising the Program, my "self" thinking is directed toward God's will for me, thoughts of character development and elimination of defects. These are good thoughts.

The Program demands that I think about myself. But it is constructive thinking, not the destructive and useless brooding on perceived wrongs.

Thinking about myself is not the problem. The problem is *how* I am thinking about myself.

With the Program disciplines baked into my life, I can avoid omphaloskepsis.

Just Do It!

The meeting topic was Step Four. One of the best shares was, "Just do it. Even if you do it wrong, you will get it right."

This principle of action, "Just do it," applies to all the Steps in our Program, but more to Step Four than the others.

Just Do It!!!

Here is part of my story.

My early attempts to conduct a moral inventory were wrong. Being arrogant, I thought I did not need any guidance from a sponsor. And being male, I did not need to read the instructions or ask for directions.

These early efforts included spreadsheets, WordPerfect bullet formats, separate lists for minor and major defects and journals. I even tried a legalistic process: I was in law school, so I drafted a Statement of Claim — "The World vs. Andy." Then, a Statement of Defence.

Finally, after exhausting all these approaches to Step Four, and still falling short of the mark, I asked my sponsor for guidance.

He suggested that I follow the instructions. I asked, "And just where, pray tell, would I find the instructions?"

Rolling his eyes (he did that often), he replied, "In the Big Book."

There they were, hiding in plain sight.

Following the instructions, my Step Four effort, I began to harvest important life-changing insights.

But looking back on my earlier misguided efforts, though wrong, they had some value that came out in later inventories. And critically, while I was trying all the wrong Step Four inventories, I stayed sober.

Just do it!!!

Even if you do it wrong, you will get it right.

Learning from Amends

With practice, we become better at making amends.

Our first amends are anxious affairs. We sweat about them, review them with our sponsors, and brace ourselves to make amends. After completing a few amends, we can relax, focus less on our fears and concerns, and become mindful of the process.

If we are mindful when we make amends, we experience not one, but two outcomes: First, we make things right, and second, we learn more about ourselves.

The first outcome is not surprising. Making amends, making things right, is the primary purpose.

The second outcome is more surprising. But surprising or not, it is genuine. When done mindfully, amends are tools of insight.

In Chapter Eight of Twelve Steps and Twelve Traditions, while discussing amends, Bill W. warms up to this theme of self-revelation. He suggests that in a well-done amend, we should extract as much information about ourselves as possible.

When making amends, we face the facts of our actions and thereby face the facts of ourselves.

First, we can see and hear the reality of what we have done and who we are. Talking with the amendee, we see and hear what we did; it is in the faces of the people with whom we are making things right.

Second, as we make amends, we see a complete picture of what transpired — what we did and the consequences. In an amend, our character defects talk back; the amendee is there to make the case. When making an amend, we often ask an amendee, "Is there anything I missed?" We get the view from the other side. We get the whole picture.

The version of my actions that plays out in my mind omits or glosses over vital elements because I suffer from the Three R's of memory: Rosy and Revisionist Recollections. When I make amends, I am confronted with the truth, unclouded by Rosy and Revisionist Recollections. The whole unclouded picture reveals more truth about myself and my character than my private inventory, no matter how carefully done.

Properly done amends are a source of self-knowledge.

PART FOUR

Program Notes

The Program of Alcoholics Anonymous is not complicated, but it is complex.

It is not difficult, but neither is it easy.

It seems trivial, but assiduously applied, it causes tremendous and momentous change.

These GEMS are thoughts on this oxymoronic theme.

Bonsai Resentments

There is a serenity garden near our home. The garden designer included a quiet meditation area, a small pool of groomed gravel, a bench, and a bonsai tree. The tree is nurtured and cared for in every detail.

With its twisted, gnarly shape, I would not call it pretty, but as I contemplated this tree one morning, I admired the pruning and shaping skill of the gardener and the beauty and balance of the final product.

Gardeners spend years of care and attention to develop a bonsai tree. They carefully prune and tie off branches to twist and grow into the desired shape. The final product is marvellous to see, and we can ponder how long and what care has been taken and the final shape is nothing like the original tree.

At a recent meeting, someone shared, "I don't just have resentments; I have bonsai resentments."

We collapsed in laughter. We knew what he was talking about.

Like a gardener with his bonsai tree, I can spend years nurturing my resentments — pruning them with affection and care, staking and tying them off so they grow into the desired twisted and gnarly shape. The resentments are not pretty, but I admire the final product. In the garden of my mind, I sit on my meditation bench, study my bonsai resentments, and consider how much time and effort I have taken with these feelings.

And, like the bonsai tree, these nurtured resentments often bear no resemblance to the original events.

With that much time invested, it is no wonder that I don't want to chop them down.

Happiness is Simple

The lady sharing must have been a teacher. She began, "Serenity is basic arithmetic, addition and subtraction."

Reality - Expectations = Serenity

"I am serene when I accept reality without expectations.

"Reality might cause me to be sad or joyful, anxious or calm. But if I have no expectations, whatever my emotional state, I will be serene. Without expectations, I am neutral to events or news; I meet life with equanimity.

"Expectations, not emotions, detract from my serenity. The amount of detraction is equal to the level of expectations. It's that simple."

Pausing to organize her thoughts, she continued, "Let me share three examples.

"For no reason at all, I am mistreated: If I had no expectation that the world would treat me well, the mistreatment would not disturb my serenity. It might offend my sense of justice, but my serenity would be unaffected. However, if I expected that everyone would treat me well, the mistreatment will disturb my serenity. The expectation is a negative drain of my serenity.

"Someone else gets the prize: If I had done my best and enjoyed the contest for its own sake, and someone else gets the prize, I might feel disappointed, but my serenity would be unaffected. But, if I expect to receive the award and the other guy gets it, the amount of my expectation will diminish my serenity.

"Something terrible happens: If I believe that I am entitled to skip merrily through the day with no bad news, if I receive bad news, my serenity will be reduced by the amount of that expectation. Without that expectation, the bad news would still be bad, I might be sad, but my serenity would be unaffected.

"As expectations increase against reality, serenity decreases; it is an iron law."

Lesson learned. Reality does not suck unless I expect that it will not suck. Without expectations, no matter what the news or events, I accept the facts and move on. It is expectations that reduce my serenity.

It is basic arithmetic, addition, and subtraction: Serenity = Reality - Expectations.

A Foolish King

From a meeting in Gulf Shores, Alabama, "With good advisors, even a foolish King can win battles."

Good advisors can give anyone an "advisor advantage."

In this GEM, let's ponder our "advisor advantages" in AA. I see at least five.

First, I have the judgments and advice of my fellow AAs. Their judgment may not always be perfect, but they are better than my old barstool companions.

Second, sometimes the best advisors are examples we can follow. The odds of seeing good examples in my AA brothers and sisters are much higher than my odds of seeing a better way of life amongst my former drinking buddies.

Third, we have sponsors and Home Groups who know our history. Knowing us and our past and possessing a sense of love and brotherly kinship, they are invaluable advisors.

Fourth, we have our Main Advisor, a Power which is greater than ourselves. As we practise the Program principles in all our affairs, we connect with our Advisor of Advisors, our Higher Power.

Finally, I can *listen* to my advisors. Sober, with a clear head and better manage feelings, I am better able to receive what my advisors have to offer. Sobriety magnifies all the other advisory advantages of the Fellowship.

Despite being a foolish King, I can win battles. Sober and in the Fellowship, I have good advisers, and I can win at the battle of life.

Fellowship to Program

There are two dimensions to Alcoholics Anonymous: The Fellowship and the Program.

In my early Program Life, I had a great Fellowship but a weak Program. If asked who my AA friends were, I could list dozens of names of AA brothers, but when asked, "What step are you working on? I had no answer."

Attending meetings, the meetings after meetings, coffee with the guys — these kept me sober.

There was more to Alcoholics Anonymous, and I was missing it. And a lot of pain was needed to get it.

I had been driven into AA by the Gift of Desperation. Troubles arising from my drinking created a sense of desperation, which forced me into the Fellowship and kept me sober. But sober and unchanged, I was a dry drunk.

To get off the dry drunk and start spiritual growth, I needed trouble. I needed a refreshed sense of desperation. I don't like trouble, and I don't want trouble. But I was grateful for trouble. With trouble, I receive a gift — the Gift of Desperation — a kick in the pants to get me going.

Let me share part of my story.

In living as a dry drunk, difficulties arose. Living with unmedicated alcoholism, trouble was sure to happen. Finally, things became difficult enough that I turned to my sponsor.

Pointing to Step Two, he instructed daily prayer on my knees. It worked — the problem dissolved with prayer.

Then later, with still more troubles, again on my sponsor's instruction, I did a Step Four inventory, took a Step Five, and then asked God to remove my defects. Applying these steps worked. I changed for the better, and as a result, the problems and pain dissolved.

After repeated experiences with the Steps and Program, I saw the pattern.

Troubles and tribulations created new sober Gifts of Desperation. Driven to ask for help by these new Gifts, I called my sponsor and followed his directions. His directions were to "apply the Steps in your life." Following this advice, I found the Program and began a Program Life.

Happily, the story does not end there. As outlined in the next GEM, eventually, I discovered growth without the touchstone of pain, without new Gifts of Desperation.

Painless Program Living

Because I was dry and unchanged, life's problems grew. Each new tribulation was another Gift of Desperation, and I was driven to apply the principles of the Program. Applying the principles in more and more of my affairs removed shortcomings and defects of character. This reduced the frequency and severity of the problems, but I still needed problems and pain to motivate me to apply the principles of the Program.

After a time, my sponsor suggested that I "try working the Program without a crisis, without a Gift of Desperation.

"Instead of waiting for the pain, take actions to maintain your spiritual condition," he suggested. "Take a year and dwell on one Step each month, whether you are in pain or not."

That year, starting in January and progressing through the twelve months, I became conscious and aware of the Steps. That started a habit of brooding on the Steps and looking for ways to apply the Steps in all my affairs. This habit is still serving me well today.

Now when I am asked, "What Step are you working on?" I have an answer.

Do you?

Not Promotion, but Attraction Takes Work

Ebby T. called on Bill W. at the Clinton Street house in Brooklyn, NY.

Bill recalls, "The door opened, and he stood there, fresh-skinned and glowing. There was something about his eyes. He was inexplicably different. What had happened?"

Ebby was attractive. Attractive enough that Bill paid attention. As a result, we have AA.

What about AA today? Are we attractive? Are we fresh-skinned and glowing? Is there something about our eyes? Do newcomers want something we have?

The wise old-timers know the importance of attraction and creating a winning impression. They get dressed for meetings and show up looking good. They look like they are succeeding, winning, and spiritually developing. They talk about problems and solutions, not problems alone. They show that this way of life can work; it really can.

Like Ebby, we should look fresh-skinned and glowing; we should have that something about our eyes. A newcomer should think, "He is inexplicably different."

We want the suffering alcoholic to ask, when they look at us, in the rooms or on the street, "What has happened? I want some of that."

Wise Old-Timers

AAs should be attractive. But there is a danger in striving to be attractive.

We are not half-measures people. We always take things to extremes. We can begin to think that we must always be attractive and look good. No matter what, we must wear a serenity game face to show that we have no problems.

But that gets old. Hiding our problems and forcing ourselves to look good is exhausting. Eventually we tire of it all and start skipping meetings and avoiding other AAs. The slide of separation from the Program has begun.

The risk is real but manageable.

Between meetings, wise old-timers keep in touch with their sponsors and each other. If they have a problem, it is first discussed privately, not publicly at meetings. And in these private conversations they see the solutions. Later, at meetings, they are ready to share both problems and solutions.

In sharing this way, these old-timers demonstrate how to show weakness and vulnerability. They can share their problems, which allows younger AAs to identify. In all areas of life, the identification process has the same power.

And they also share stories of the solutions. In so doing, they show hope, not despair.

Old-timers work between meetings to be attractive at meetings.

Dance Steps

There is a life lesson to be learned in ballroom dancing.

The lesson? Dancers affect each other. That is the nature of dancing. That, too, is the nature of daily life.

A dancer reflects his partner's moves. If a dancer does something, his partner will react to that move. This is true whether the dancing partner is cheek-to-cheek or far away across the dance floor. Any change by one partner triggers a change by the other.

We all affect each other. In a dance or in life, if I change, the others in my orbit change.

The interdependencies are easy to see in close situations. If I snap at my wife, she'll respond stiffly, but if I change my manner and greet my wife with a warm smile, a different, more pleasant reaction will ensue. She will change to match my mood and moves.

We can see similar interdependencies in more distant situations. If I decide to drive my car aggressively, other drivers sense it and drive aggressively as well, but if I change and let someone in front of me, everyone seems to drive better.

In life, this phenomenon of change - inducing - change extends to the whole world. It applies in the specifics of life, like spousal conversations or driving to work, and applies equally to the general case, the approach that I bring to life.

If I approach the world with a sense of entitlement, it will reply with antagonism. But if I change and replace my sense of entitlement with gratitude, the world does not seem so angry. If I believe that life is maltreating me, people tend to fulfill that prophecy and push me away. But if I change and come to believe that God is in charge and His world is unfolding in accordance with His design, the world changes and seems grateful to have me around.

Disciplined by the Program, I change for the better, and the world around me changes as well.

Life is like a ballroom dance.

Ethyl Was a Great Old Girl

An AA friend shared this at a recent meeting: "Ethyl... Ethyl Alcohol, I remember her well. She was a good old girl. She made me feel good and gave me some great memories. Then she turned ugly. She beat me into submission and stole everything that I had. She and her cousin John Barleycorn did a tag team that brought me to my knees.

"Every time I invited Ethyl and John into my life, they took over, and it went bad; I had to kick them out to save myself.

"It was not their fault; it was not my fault either; I was wired that way. It was a chemical reaction, not an issue of morality. Millions of others welcome John and Ethyl into their lives, without any issues.

"Finally, I accepted that I react badly whenever Ethyl or John come into my life. I had to ask them to leave and deny them entry to my life, one day at a time. It was hard work; damn, they were persistent, cunning, and powerful. And seeing everyone else get along with them made the job more difficult.

"I benefited from knowing them, difficult as they were. The pain and suffering they brought, and the work to get rid of them, paid off handsomely. Because of the failed relationship with Ethyl and John, I am on a spiritual path, with new friends and companions. I no longer want or need the company of Ethyl and John; nothing against them; they just don't work for me."

He concluded, "And my new spiritual friends, Al Truism and Hy Power, are great buddies to have in my life; they are much better company."

Desire Versus Willingness

"The only requirement for attendance at an AA meeting is a desire to stop drinking, but the requirement for full membership is a willingness to change."

This share "rang my bell."

When I arrived at the doors of AA, I met the requirement for attendance at an AA meeting; I had a desire to stop drinking. However, I did not have the requirement for full membership yet; I was not willing to change.

When I first came to the Rooms, I did not want to change and did not think I had to change.

I thought I would automatically stay sober by hanging out with my new AA friends and going to meetings. Easy peasy. AA was my new social network. That would solve all my problems.

I had reached this brilliant conclusion within 30 days of my first meeting. I was a pigeon prodigy.

My new friends and going to meetings allowed me to become "dry." But dryness is not sobriety. Phrases like "Go to meetings and don't drink between," "Sit in a barber's chair, and you'll get a haircut, go to a bar, and you'll get a drink," or "Winners stick with winners," were my principles. And this was good, as far as it went.

But as time passed, I came to see fellow AAs who had contented sobriety and had acquired characteristics, such as calm, measured, and serene living. I did not have these. Instead, I was tense, rash and anxious. I was dry but not sober, because it did not occur to me that I would have to change.

After a time, the Fellowship and meetings led to Steps, and Steps led to change.

Now I meet the requirements for attendance and full membership; I have a desire to stop drinking and a willingness to change.

It Is Difficult to Learn Something When You Know It All

"It is difficult to learn anything when I know it all."

To learn something, I have to get it into my head; if "I know it all," my head is full, there is no room left.

Sometimes my head is full because of my superior status; I am high above the common crowd, and I see things more clearly than lesser mortals. There is no need for more information or other perspectives. I know and understand all the relevant facts. In my superiority, all the space in my head is taken; it is completely full. As a result, anything you tell me goes into my ears and overflows onto the floor.

Other times, my head is full, and I know it all because I have intuited the conclusion. I don't have to hear all the evidence, and I conclude that I have heard enough. At that point, "I know it all." I have thought about the matter and reached my conclusion. I have filled my brain, and anything you tell me overflows onto the floor.

Could this unhappy state get any worse? Yes! This unfortunate state is amplified because when I am in this condition. I don't know that I know it all. I am blind to my attitude of "I know it all."

There is only one way to make more room in my head. Life picks me up, shakes me, and then tips me over to pour some stuff from my head to make room for new knowledge or information.

Getting picked up and shaken, then tipped over is painful but seems to be the only way to clear some space for new knowledge.

It is difficult when "I know it all."

PART FIVE

Program Goals and Habits

In life, we always have goals.

We can consciously select goals, or our subconscious will do it for us. Nature abhors a vacuum; if we don't identify a goal, our minds automatically fill the vacuum and select a goal. It might be good, or it might be bad.

We have different categories of goals: career goals, sports goals, education goals, family goals, and Program goals.

In a Program Life, wherever we are in our sobriety, we will have goals. And like other categories of goals, Program goals are developed either consciously or unconsciously, and can be either good or bad.

There are conscious Program goals. For example, when I came into the Program, I was aware of the desire to stay sober.

And there are unconscious Program goals. Looking back on my Program Life, I can see I unconsciously formed a goal of "having a spiritual awakening." The habitual reading of *How It Works* subliminally created a Step Twelve goal, a spiritual awakening.

Conscious or unconscious, selecting good goals is critical. I have chosen both good and bad goals, sometimes consciously and, at other times, unconsciously. I cannot guarantee that I will always select good goals, but I can create a tendency towards choosing good goals, rather than bad.

Over the years, I have noticed that I tend to choose good life goals if I have good living habits. Living habits like adequate sleep, a balanced diet, and making my bed in the morning incline me toward good life goals, consciously or unconsciously.

Likewise, consciously and unconsciously, I tend to select good Program goals if I have good Program habits. Good Program habits, like going to meetings, sponsoring others, and service work. Good Program habits incline me towards good Program goals.

In regular life and Program Life, good habits lead to good goals, both consciously and unconsciously developed.

These Gems are stories and meditations on Program goals and the supporting Program habits.

Look Where You Want to Go

Watch where you are looking, because where you are looking is where you will go.

A beginner skydiver landed in the wet and soggy corner of the landing field, missing the bull's eye marking the solid and dry target area. When his instructors picked him up with his bedraggled and sodden parachute, he said, "How did I end up here in this swamp? I focused on staying away from it."

The instructor said, "You were probably looking at the swamp, rather than the bull's eye. Look at where you want to land because where you look is where you land."

In a shopping mall parking lot late at night, with only two trucks on the ten-acre lot, one truck ran into the other. The driver told the police, "I don't know how this happened. All I had to do was drive around the other truck, and there was lots of room on either side. I was looking at it to avoid it, and bang, I ran into it."

The officer said, "You should have been looking at the space beside the truck, not the truck itself, because where you are looking is where you will drive."

Like a skydiver or a truck driver, where we look is where we go.

Our lives will go where we are looking, where we are mentally paying attention. What we are thinking about will come to pass.

In parachuting, driving, and life, what we pay attention to is where we end up. If we focus on sex, we shape our characters accordingly. If we concentrate on money, it will dominate us. If we are looking to God, we will draw closer to Him. If we concentrate on serving others, we will reap the rewards.

So, pay attention to where you are looking because that's where you will go.

Conversely, pay attention to where you are because that is where you have been looking. If you are in a swamp, that's where your attention is focused.

Our Special Fear

From a Joe and Charlie tape, "One of the hallmarks of a life run on self-will is fear."

Joe and Charlie could have added, "Self-will fear is a special kind of fear." Special in two ways.

When I am running on self-will, fear comes upon me sooner, and when it comes, it goes deeper into my soul.

Self-willed fear comes sooner.

If I am spiritually fit, I don't feel fear until reality and life become dangerous. Then fear is useful for guidance and response, arising when I need it. Fear is warranted and actionable; I am dealing with reality. When I am running on self-will, it comes sooner, long before I need it.

There is a reason why this is so; if I am self-willed, my imagination creates fear of failure long before it happens. I believe everything depends on me and my resources. Looking at the world through this lens, aware of my frailties and weaknesses, I imagine failure long before the possibility of failure.

Fear comes sooner.

And self-willed fear goes deeper into my soul.

If I am spiritually fit, I am consciously aware of my Higher Power. I feel I can deal with all outcomes; He is in charge.

When I am running on self-will, it is deeper because the universe is all about me and my wishes. Failure means that the world is not unfolding as I have wished. Because it is all about me, failure is not a trivial problem; it is an existential threat. I have willed something to be so, and it is not working out; my willpower is being denied. This denial of my power creates a deep fear, a fear that goes to my core.

Yes, fear is a hallmark of a self-willed life, and it is a special fear. It is both faster and deeper.

Humorous, Practical Zen

A share at a meeting: "Being present in the moment can make for a long day. It is amazing how long the day is when you're there for the whole thing."

It struck us as funny, but the insight was practical as well as humorous.

She continued her share, "The day does not seem longer because the time is dragging; it seems longer because I am more effective and efficient. When I am in the moment, an hour is more productive than an hour spent not living in the here and now. The same 60-minute period has a higher yield and output.

"Being present and in the moment, I am focusing on what is in front of me; what I am doing is fascinating. Fascination leads to concentration, which leads to efficiency. And when I am more efficient, there is more than enough time to do everything that needs doing.

"Living in the moment, I focus on what is essential and disregard the non-essential. I more readily identify the things that I can change and more easily ignore the rest. Ignoring the non-essential and accepting the things I cannot change saves emotional and mental energy. I am more productive."

"And this is not a theoretical benefit; I know it to be true.

"I have seen one of the benefits of being in the moment in meetings at work. All of us spend a lot of time in meetings. I used to focus on what I was going to say. But if I am in a meeting and in a state of mindful awareness, I don't worry about myself. I don't worry about what I am going to say or how I look. Instead, I concentrate on what the speaker is saying and how the participants are receiving it. If the subject is controversial, I can sense the undercurrents of the meeting and more clearly see everyone's agendas involved. It seems that all the motives are laid out before me. I intuitively know how to handle situations that used to baffle me, and I am blessed with a relaxed sense of energy."

It was a great share. Being present in the moment makes for a long day: funny and practical spiritual advice.

We Lie to Newcomers

"You will never be given more than you can handle."

We often use this line with newcomers; it is comforting for them to hear when they are in trouble, and things are not going well.

But there is a problem. It is false! We are often given more than we can handle. For example, alcohol was more than I could handle.

I was given two alcoholic characteristics, one physical and one mental.

The physical, an allergic reaction. Once I had started, I could not stop.

The mental, as I took my first drink, my mental quirk quirked. I forgot all my previous drinking experiences.

And this combination was beyond my control. With my allergic reaction to alcohol and my peculiar mental twist, I had been given more than I could handle.

And there is more. After I sobered up, many character defects appeared, and they were more than I could handle. Pride, sex, anger, and fear were instincts I could not control. They all created problems. Again, I was given more than I could handle.

The truth is, I am often given more than I can handle.

We are telling the newcomer a small lie when we say, "You will never be given more than you can handle." But the lie will be forgiven. In due course, the newcomer will see the good news in being given more than he can handle.

This is the good news: When we are given more than we can handle, we are driven to ask for help, and when we ask for help, help will always come. Help comes from the Fellowship, the Program, and *God as I have understood Him.* Each "help" is further evidence of love, and each demonstration of love is another spiritual awakening.

We get better because we are given more than we can handle.

In due course, the newcomer, given more than he can handle, will feel the love that comes from asking for help and he will forgive our deceit, and in turn, lie to another newcomer.

Impression Management

The opposite of self-esteem is other-esteem. Self-esteem is feeling good because I think I am good. Other-esteem is the feeling good because I think you think I am good. This is why I crave your approval. I depend on what you think of me for the esteem I want to feel.

Other-esteem requires management of the image that I am presenting to you, because the only way I can think well of myself, to have some sense of esteem, is to convince you to think well of me. All my mental, spiritual, and emotional energies are focused with laser-like intensity on one thing — making sure that I am presenting the right image.

The complexity of this task is astounding. It includes how I look, how I think you feel, what is happening around us, and all the vagaries of the moment. Impression management is a difficult job, requiring my complete attention.

For example, when I first meet you, you will tell me your name, but your name will not enter my consciousness because I am ruthlessly focused on the image I am projecting to you. Before I have any interest in your name, I need to know that I have suitably impressed you.

Then it is too late. I missed your name.

I have to ask you again for your name. I blame my poor memory, but I should apologize for my desperate desire for your approval arising from my lack of self-esteem.

And after we have sorted out each other's names, we have a conversation. As our conversation progresses, I work hard to continue to project the right image, an image of success. As the gap grows between the outer appearance of success and my internal sense of unworthiness, so grows the fear that I will be found out.

You can see why a simple introduction and conversation is, for me, exhausting.

The key to solving this problem is in our Program. As promised in Step Twelve, as a result of working our Program, I had spiritual awakenings.

With each spiritual awakening, I improved my view of myself. I realized that I am a child of God. I developed self-respect. I became less dependent on what I think you think of me.

One of the consequences of doing the Steps is self-esteem.

This is a much better way to live, and I might even remember your name.

Emotional Balance

I took up the sport of tennis late in life. I hired a coach who had life wisdom as well as tennis skills.

One morning we were practising. I missed an easy shot. Angry, I stamped my feet and swore under my breath.

My coach stopped and walked up to the net. He waved his hand, calling me over.

He looked at his racquet as I walked to the centre of the court to where he was waiting. I could not get a read on what was coming. I thought maybe it was a tip on my strokes.

It was much more valuable than a tip on strokes. He looked up and said to me, "Okay, that is enough of that. If you have a temper tantrum when you miss a shot, you must display an equal amount of happiness when you make a good shot. So, you can choose. Either take everything in stride or match the swearing and foot-stomping with jumps of joy."

He paused and finished, saying, "Trust me, you don't have enough energy to do both, so you better learn to deal with the odd mistake."

Message delivered, he turned and walked back to the baseline.

Wow, here I am, 55 years old, and I am getting a lecture on emotional balance from a tennis coach.

But what a beautiful moment. He had hit on something. He was right; I had no balance. Negatives were real, positives ephemeral. Negatives were enormous; positives were trivial. Anything negative in my life was 10 or 20 times the weight of anything positive.

One "sad face" would ruin a series of "happy faces." I could have a great week; then, one thing would go wrong on Friday afternoon, and in my mind, the whole week would be a write-off. One bad moment was proof that I was incompetent, incapable of doing anything, and a thoroughly worthless person.

Small wonder, I consistently responded in anger to even a tiny adverse event. If it was negative, it was huge.

Through a tennis coach, I saw my lack of proportion and began the journey to balance.

I have learned to practise these principles in all my affairs, even while playing tennis.

Conscious Awareness and a New Forehand

In the preceding GEM, I described a spiritual lesson learned from my tennis coach. I have learned other lessons in tennis, like this one.

My forehand was not a bad stroke, but my coach said, "It could be much better with a small change."

I saw other players using the technique my coach recommended. It was working for them, and I trusted my coach. So, I decided to adopt the change.

But changing a tennis stroke is difficult.

The old forehand was familiar and comfortable. In pressure situations, I reverted to the old.

I knew the new technique — I had practised it and seen the results — but knowledge is not enough. In a high-pressure moment, the old technique came back.

Using the new stroke and breaking the old habit required focus, and sometimes I lost focus. I might be paying attention to the score or worrying about how I look on the court; whatever the reason, I would lose focus for a split second, and unconsciously revert to the old ways.

Sometimes the new stroke felt awkward. The movement felt forced and unnatural. Uncomfortable, I would revert to the familiar habit of the old forehand. It felt more natural.

And the new stroke occasionally misfired. It was new. I would not complete the stroke correctly, and with the occasional bad outcome, I began to doubt the whole effort.

For all these reasons, changing a tennis stroke takes a long time and a lot of discipline. It is not an overnight project.

Changing my spiritual habits was like changing my forehand.

My sponsor suggested a new technique for living: "Rather than trust in your judgment, rely on a conscious awareness of God; pause and ask Him for directions."

I trusted my sponsor, almost as much as my tennis coach. I could see the benefits of the new approach he suggested, and I could see that it was used successfully by my fellow AAs.

But like a new forehand, this new way of approaching life was difficult to habituate.

Forming my opinion on something and forging ahead, the old way of handling problems, was familiar and comfortable. I knew pausing and turning to my Higher Power was a good idea. But knowledge was not enough.

In pressure situations, the old self-willed habits slipped into gear.

Learning to pause and turn to God required focus, and sometimes I lost focus.

At other times, when I was focused, it seemed awkward to trust in an intuition that might or might not have come from God. It felt forced and risky.

Lastly, I experienced odd results in the early days of this new way of acting. The occasional misfire cast doubt on the new process.

But pushing through the problems of changing my tennis strokes improved my game. It took hundreds of strokes and lots of practice, but it was worth it. Developing a habit of pausing and turning to God improved my life. It took hundreds of decisions and a lot of practice, but it was worth it. My life improved.

We take lessons from all our affairs and practise these principles in all our affairs, including tennis.

Fear, Hope To Joy

We start with fear. Dr. Silkworth told Bill, "Give them the straight goods about their drinking and the hopelessness of their condition."

With newcomers, fear is our ally; we tell them, "Continue to drink, and the only options are death, institutions, or insanity."

We offer our stories of drinking. By sharing our stories, we allow them to identify with us. Using our past fears, we help them identify and find their fears, find their bottom.

Fear motivates and compels the newcomer to take actions he does not believe or understand. Actions we know will result in recovery. We can frighten the newcomer into taking the required steps, and for many, it works.

Some struggle because they are not afraid enough, but in others, we see enough fear to overcome the belief that they can "lick the problem alone." They have hit a solid bottom; they have been given the Gift of Desperation; fear has done its job.

Fear is a start. Next comes hope.

Again, using our stories, we show by our recovery, and the recovery of thousands of others, that it works. Hope replaces fear.

Past hope is joy. If we are in a fit spiritual condition, we demonstrate that life can be full of joy. We have friends and experience true happiness and freedom. These are not extravagant promises. Sometimes quickly and sometimes slowly, the Program Life becomes joyful. Again, with the process of identification, they come to believe that they might have joy as well.

At this point, they are participating Members of AA, and the story begins anew. The newcomer grows and, with God, shapes a new character. Soon our newcomer is working with others and using fear to create a bottom for them.

We can watch our former pigeons with future newcomers, and re-live the magic, from fear, through hope, to joy.

Plant Your Pole and Fly

People wear T-shirts that broadcast interests and affiliations. Recently, a fellow showed up at a meeting with a T-shirt which read:

How To Pole Vault

1. Approach the bar running

2. Plant your Pole

3. Take off into the air

4. Swing your body up

5. Extend your body

6. Turn your body

7. Then fly away

My first impression was, "That is an odd T-shirt to wear to an AA meeting."

But then the member wearing the T-shirt shared and changed my opinion. It was a great T-shirt to wear to an AA meeting.

The member shared, "The author of this shirt has broken pole-vaulting into a sequence of simple steps.

"There are seven basic steps. First, imagine a pole vaulter at the end of the runway, pole balanced, and bouncing on his toes. He starts running towards the bar. Then he completes the remaining six steps.

"He must take each step fearlessly and thoroughly. If the pole vaulter hesitates as he runs, he will not have enough speed. He will run into the safety net if he balks at planting the pole in the pole-catching block. He must be fully committed as he takes off, swings up, extends and turns. To achieve a successful outcome, he must be thorough, fully committed and hold nothing back; he must leap, twist, and extend his body.

"And there is a correct sequence. If the vaulter leaps before planting his pole, he will end up in the landing pad, a tangled mess of poles, bars, and cleats.

If he plants his pole before he starts running, he goes nowhere. The sequence is critical.

"The steps must be taken fearlessly, thoroughly and in the correct sequence.

He continued, "Sobriety is like pole vaulting.

"There is a series of Twelve Steps, and each Step must be taken fearlessly and thoroughly. If we are afraid and hold back, we often pay with a relapse.

In our Program, there is a sequence. Doing Step Nine amends before completing Steps One through Eight often goes badly, so badly we have to go back and make amends for the amends."

He wrapped up, "If you don't follow the steps in pole vaulting, you will not clear the bar. In sobriety, if we don't follow the Steps in our Program, we will not get out of the bar."

Love Yourself Someday

Recently at a meeting, a returnee tearfully talked about how he had almost killed himself. I thought back to my first suicide ideation. I was 15 years old. Even then, I was full of self-loathing and self-doubt. But I did not see it for what it was.

I began practicing the Steps. By doing an inventory, I learned a simple but hidden truth: I hated myself. In my inventory, I unveiled this self-hatred.

I had spent time thinking about myself before AA. I would spend hours dwelling on myself and my victimhood. That got me nowhere. But thinking about myself within the Steps was different. Thinking about myself in Step Four was structured, disciplined and revealingly effective.

Discovering my self-loathing, I needed to do something. Character defects were the problem. I did not see this when I started; I learned this when I followed the Steps.

The next Step was shortcomings. Shortcomings had to be removed. With the removal of each defect, another blockage was eliminated, allowing the sunlight of the spirit and its healing rays to brighten my soul. In this sunlight, I grew from self-loathing to self-love.

Through these processes, I came to see my self-loathing, and through working the Steps, it diminished.

Following the Program suggestions, I came to value my life. I came to a state of proper self-love.

How Good a Friend is God?

A fellow wearing a fishing hat at our AA meeting made a comment which showed that all the time he spent on the water was not thoughtless time.

The topic of the meeting was, "Our relationship with God."

He said, "If I claim a relationship with God, what does it say about that relationship if all I do is give him a quick hello in the morning and a passing 'good night' as I go to sleep?"

Our friend continued, "If I don't talk with Him during the day, can my relationship be that meaningful? It seems to me, if I have a meaningful relationship with God, I will talk with Him during the day. I will ask for His thoughts and opinions. I will share my life with Him."

Wow, what a great truth.

A relationship's depth is, in part, reflected in the frequency of the interactions between the parties. A morning "hello" and an evening "goodbye," with nothing in between, day after day, suggests a trivial relationship.

Hellos and goodbyes are essential. They keep things running smoothly. But how serious is the connection if that is all that is going on?

In my relationship with my Higher Power, I must remember to say, "good morning" and "good night"; that is a great beginning and end to the day. But I should not forget to ask Him during the day: "What do you think? How am I doing?"

During the day, it behooves me to show some interest in what my Higher Power thinks and what guidance He might give.

PART SIX

Personal Program Observations

T hese GEMS are thoughts, gathered along my Program journey.

God Is Not My Fix-it-Fairy

The Turf men's meeting is one of the oldest meetings in Calgary. A range of AAs attend, from downtown lawyers and bankers to street gang bikers. Cross-talk is the norm, and there is a low tolerance for whining. The Chairman has a plastic baby bottle, and if someone shares about feeling sorry for them-selves for too long, the Chairman will toss the baby bottle to him, with the suggestion that he "suck on that for a while."

As I said, tough. But loving. And centuries of sobriety.

One Thursday night, at a regular meeting, a fellow shared.

Some of us knew him from other meetings. He started by saying that he had been in the Program for a while, but this was the first time he had attend-ed the Turf. That night, he was on the self-pity pot. Feeling put upon, oppressed, and angry, he felt he had to share his misery.

He went on for some time. He said, "I have never been to this meeting, but I needed someone to listen. I have been sober for a while, but I feel betrayed by my Higher Power.

"God has not answered my prayers. I prayed to God, but my wife is still difficult, and my boss is an idiot."

We let him finish. The baby bottle was reserved for regulars. But we heard him loud and clear; God was not treating him right, God was letting him down, and God had not fixed things to our friend's specifications.

A well-dressed banker spoke next. His contribution was polite and well-intentioned. He said, referring to the earlier share, "You are in the right place; keep coming back."

The next share was different. He was huge. With motorcycle boots, a Harley-Davidson vest, and a leather cap, he contrasted dramatically with the well-dressed banker. He leaned forward, looked across the table at the complainer and growled, "You have been around for a while. You should know that God is not some sort of Fix-It-Fairy."

He leaned back, "That's all."

Hearing this hulking example of the biking culture talking about a little fairy on gossamer wings was hilarious. We had a good laugh.

It was funny, but he made a serious point. God, as I have understood Him, is not a Fix-It Fairy.

He does not sprinkle pixie dust and make my problems disappear. He does not flutter by on gossamer wings and remove all my problems. He does not wave a magic wand and change everyone who irritates me.

As I have understood Him, God is not a "Fix-It-Fairy," who makes my circumstances perfect.

Nor is God a 'Fix-*Me*-Fairy.'

He does not sprinkle pixie dust or wave a wand and transform me. He has given me the Steps, and I have to take them. I have to put in the "hard yards."

I must do an inventory. After that, I have to book a Fifth Step to review my defects of character and shortcomings. Then, I have to pray to have these removed.

God may direct us, like a father, a director, or an employer, but we must do the work.

So, the biker was right in saying God is not a Fix-It-Fairy. And the new guy, he laughed with us. He is now a regular at the Turf.

My "Understooding" of God

In his AA talks, the late Cec. Corrigall, from Saskatchewan, frequently told his audiences to pay attention to the difference between "understood" and "understand."

In the Steps, it says, "God as we *understood* Him," not "God as we *understand* Him." We use the past tense, not the present tense.

What genius Bill W. and the old-timers possessed in writing the Big Book. That difference, from present tense, understand, to the past tense, understood, is enormous. They could have said, "God as I *understand* Him," but they did not. By using the word, *understood*, they shifted the entire meaning.

God, *as I understood Him* — the past tense — is my history with God. It refers to my personal experience of God. The story of my relationship with Him is my "understooding" of God.

In contrast, my understanding of God — the present tense — includes my thoughts, theories, and beliefs about God. My understanding of God is my opinion of how God works.

My understandings of God are my ideas about God. My "understoodings" of God are my experiences of God.

Listen to AAs talk about God. They talk about the God that saved them or the Power that rescued them from disaster or death. They talk about their lives and the coincidences that are too coincidental to be coincidental. They talk about the role that God has played in work, family, and spiritual progress. These are all experiences, stories — his-stories and her-stories with God.

They don't share current theories of God or debate whether God is immanent or transcendent. AAs share their past experiences with God.

We share our "understooding" of God: what it was like, what happened and what it is like now, with God.

If the Founders had used *understand* instead of *understood*, AA meetings would focus on metaphysical claptrap, talking about God's mechanics.

Instead, we talk about our experience of God. And that is good.

The Heart Is a Divine Antenna

At last week's meeting, someone shared, "The heart is an antenna for the divine."

She continued, "Electromagnetic radio waves are moving through the ether all the time, though you cannot see or hear them. A radio antenna picks up electromagnetic waves, and the electrons in the antenna vibrate in sympathy with the invisible electromagnetic waves.

"Even an antenna that is not connected to anything will vibrate in sympathy with the radio signals in the air, but it will do no good. The antenna's electrons may vibrate, but the vibrations go nowhere. But, if you connect the antenna to a radio turned on and tuned to the correct channel, the vibrations will be converted to intelligible music.

"Sometimes the radio needs work; the sound goes silent or becomes garbled. The electromagnetic waves are still there, and the antenna is still vibrating. The problem is with the radio. I have to check the tuning and the power connections of the radio. I might even have to run a repair protocol on the radio.

"God's messages are like electromagnetic radio waves; they are always there even though you cannot see or hear them. My heart, my spiritual antenna, will vibrate in sympathy with the waves, even if it is unconnected, but these vibrations are useless unless my mind is connected to the antenna, turned on and tuned right.

"If my heart and mind are not connected, nothing happens; the spiritual vibrations don't go anywhere. And if my mind is not turned on and tuned to the right channel, the waves will be garbled and distorted.

"There are times when all I have heard through my divine antenna is silence or static. At first, I blamed God. But His spiritual waves are always there. No, I was the problem; it was time to do a maintenance check. First, the connection between my heart and mind might be blocked. I may need to remove a shortcoming. Next, is the power turned on? Maybe I need to meditate and become conscious of

God. Then, I should check the tuning: have I turned my will and my life to His care and protection?

"Properly connected, tuned, and in good repair, I hear the spiritual waves loud and clear."

She was right; the heart is a divine antenna, and that is just the beginning.

Waking up SOBER

When we sober up and face life, we realize that S.O.B.E.R.

"<u>S</u>on <u>O</u>f a <u>B</u>itch, <u>E</u>verything is <u>R</u>eal!"

I did not like anything to be real; I was attracted to fiction and avoided reality. Fictions like, *everyone is out to get me*, and *it is not my problem* were more attractive than, *I am not that important*, and *I am responsible.*

To avoid reality, I drank. It was my solution to avoiding anything real. And I went to great lengths to apply this tool.

Coming to AA and living without booze, I lost my drinking avoidance tool. Still not liking reality, I developed new reality avoidance tools to help me avoid either being real or facing reality. Since I was sober, they were my sober reality avoidance tools.

One oft-used sober reality avoidance tool was my bad temper. Whether I was on the tennis court or in a boardroom, whenever I lost, I would curse, swear, and stamp my feet.

Blame was another sober reality avoidance tool. If I failed at anything, I blamed life, partners, staff, or the world for the wrongs done to me.

If I was bored with reality, I would turn to inappropriate websites, compulsive eating, or excessive exercise.

I stopped drinking, but still, I did not like reality, and to deal with reality, I applied my avoidance tools — bad behaviours.

Persisting in the Steps, I saw these immature self-possessed behaviours for what they were: reality avoidance tools to replace booze.

With this realization, I saw I was refusing to get real or face reality. And it got personal; I also realized I did not like the real me.

Continuing to persist in applying the principles of the Program, I learned to deal with reality and put reality avoidance tools away. I accepted reality. And I also learned to accept and love myself.

Today, I face the simple and obvious truth: S.O.B.E.R., Son Of a Bitch, Everything is Real.

I turn to my Higher Power for help and get on with the day.

Is There More to Life?

I was working with Chris, a new pigeon.

In an early session, he said, "There is more to my life than me."

I remember thinking, wow, only 60 days sober, and he comes up with that. "Out of the mouths of babes! He's right; my life is much more than me."

In my life, booze was a problem. As Bill W. said, I find my solution to this problem on two planes: spiritual and altruistic.

In both planes, "There is more to my life than me."

In the spiritual plane, there is "more than me;" there is a Higher Power.

On the altruistic plane, I serve others, and the others are "more than me."

In addition, the other parts of my life are "more than me."

The joys of life are friends and family, the relationships that make up my life. The richness and texture of my life come from outside of me; again, there is more than me.

My actions have an effect outside of me. The results of my life, good or bad, are more than me. I think of the services that I have performed. I think of the harms and wrongs that I have done. My actions and words affect many others. There are many consequences outside and beyond me.

And my life is built on others: parents who brought me into this world and nurtured me, teachers who taught me lessons, clients or employers who gave me sustenance in return for services. There is way more than me.

Thank you, Chris. "There is more to my life than me."

Kicking the Bottle
Down the Road

I was new in the Program. I went to my Thursday meeting, the Hill Group in Toronto.

My sponsor's sponsor stood next to me in the coffee line after the meeting. Being an old-timer, he quickly got down to business. "Your sponsor and I have been talking; we are worried that you are just kicking the bottle down the road."

"What do you mean?" I asked.

"Here is what I mean," he said, "You are sober, and that is good, but you kick the bottle down the road a bit, walk up to it, stop, look down, and think about it for a while; then you kick it again. You kick, follow, pause; kick, follow, pause, over and over.

"Sooner or later, you will bend down and pick it up instead of kicking it away."

"Well," I replied, "What should I be doing?"

"Turn around and walk away, walk in the other direction, and you do that by working the Steps."

He may have saved my life. I stopped kicking the bottle out in front, following it, pausing, then kicking it again. Working the Steps, I turned around and walked the other way, away from the bottle.

You might ask, "Why would you still remember that conversation from so many years ago?"

I remember it because I have used the pattern of kick, follow, pause, and kick, again and again — not with booze, but with my shortcomings and character defects.

I use the kick, follow, pause, and kick, follow, pause pattern with my character defects in all my affairs.

With one shortcoming after another, I kick it out in front. Feeling smug, I say to myself, "There, it is away from me."

Then I walk up to it, pause, and look down at it. Every once in a while, instead of kicking it, I will pick it up and play with it for a while, then in disgust, kick it down the road; follow it once more and pause and look down.

Sometimes I pick it up; sometimes, I kick it. But I don't get rid of it.

I don't get rid of it, till one day, sick and tired of that defect, I begin practising the Program's principles and, with God's good grace, turn around and walk the other way by applying the Steps to the problem.

Normal Is a Setting

Recently, at the Welcome Group in Thunder Bay, a newcomer complained, "I just want to be normal."

The next speaker chuckled when he said, "Normal is a setting on the dryer."

This bit of humour contains a truth. Our Program promises sobriety, not normality. Practising these principles in all our affairs, we will have a sober life, not a normal life.

If AA promised a normal life, our meetings would be debates about what is "normal."

Normal is a general pattern of behaviour. When people talk about normal, they talk about opinions and beliefs. They are talking about what "most people" might find acceptable.

Normal involves too many opinions. Alcoholics arguing about what is normal is not a good idea. We have trouble agreeing on a brand of coffee for our meetings.

But we don't have to worry because we are promised sober, not normal. There is no discussion about what is normal; there are only discussions of sobriety. That starts with "no drinking." There is no debate. Either you are, or you are not drinking. Later, as an AA, I strive for maturity, sobriety, and spiritual growth. I do not attempt to be normal. Instead, I focus on being mature and consciously aware of God.

Thank goodness that Bill and Bob did not aspire to normality; they were only after sobriety. They understood that, for Alcoholics of our type, "Normal is best thought of as a setting on a dryer."

Bathing is Lonely

I remember a movie, years ago, "Arthur," featuring Dudley Moore as Arthur. Arthur was a wealthy New York drunk. He lived a life of indolent luxury in a palatial apartment on Central Park. And he drank like a fish.

One morning, after a particularly bad evening, the butler, Hobson, played by Sir John Gielgud, drew a hot bath for the desperately hungover Arthur. Soaking in the luxurious bubbles, he said mournfully, through his alcohol haze, "I feel so alone."

Hobson, a very correct and polite English butler, was folding a plush towel. He replied, "Yes, Master Arthur, bathing is a lonely endeavour." Having said his piece, he hung the towel, turned and left the room.

People in a bath are usually alone. And in a way, sobriety is like bathing. Everyone who is sober is alone; each individual has his or her own journey. We don't have a collective story; we have individual stories.

But at this point, the similarity between bathing and sobriety ends. Taking a bath, I am both alone and lonely, but in my Program, I am alone, but not lonely. "We do together that which I cannot do on my own."

Sobriety is a personal journey, and in this journey, I am alone, but not lonely; I am with my alcoholic brothers and sisters.

God's Grace and Grits

We had just arrived for our first holiday at Gulf Shores, Alabama. It was Sunday. My wife and I stopped for breakfast and experienced a quintessential Southern moment.

The waitress came over, coffee pot in hand, and with a friendly smile, said, "Good morning to you all. Isn't this a fine morning?" Without waiting for a reply, assuming agreement, she continued, "Would you like some coffee to start? By the way, if you need anything, call out 'Alice,' and I will be there for you."

With that enormous greeting out of the way, we ordered breakfast and started to enjoy our coffee. The shop was busy with customers. Most were well-dressed, just coming back from church. A few had well-worn Bibles under their arms. We were clearly in the deep south.

Our new-found friend, Alice, came back with our food.

As she laid my wife's plate first, I noticed a peculiar substance beside the bacon. The same material was on my plate as well. "Alice," I inquired, "What is this?" pointing to the gruel.

"Well, honey, those are grits."

"Interesting. They were not on the list of ingredients on the menu."

"Well dear, this is the South. You don't have to want grits; you don't have to ask for grits; you just get grits." Then, without any hesitation, suggesting a deep familiarity with the sentiment, she continued, "Just like God's good grace. You don't have to want God's grace; you don't have to ask for God's good grace; you just get His mercy and grace. The only difference being, I like my grits with butter, God's grace, I like plain."

Laughing at her own spiritual humour, she turned to another table, "Good morning to you all; this is a fine morning."

Well, Alice was right; the grits were good. Better with butter.

And she was right about God's grace as well. You don't have to want it; you don't have to ask for it; you just get it."

How I See Is What I See

My wife and I were on a driving holiday. She was the navigator; I was driving. She called out, "There's the sign for our turnoff."

I could see a highway sign but could not read the words. I said, "How can you know that?"

She turned to me and, with a look that suggested more pity than affection, said, "Can't you read the sign?"

I could not read the sign. Up till that point, I thought my vision was fine. I was wrong.

When I got home, I booked an eye exam. The optometrist said I needed glasses for distance. Over the years, my eyesight had changed, and I had not noticed.

After a few days, I picked up my new glasses. I tried them on and was amazed at the change. Distant objects that had been hazy and obscure were now clear and bright. As I reported to my wife, "Driving home, I could see traffic lights three blocks away. It was amazing."

My glasses did not change the outside world, but they changed how I perceived it. The lenses in my glasses bend the light that comes into my eyes, which changes the information my brain processes. The result is improved vision. I could see well enough to get by with my old glasses, but my new glasses improved my perception of the world.

Attitudes and beliefs are like lenses in my glasses. Lenses bend the light, the information that comes into my eyes. Attitudes and beliefs bend the information that comes into my heart.

I have lived with notions like "The world revolves around me," "I know everything," "I don't need God," and "The world is against me" for most of my life.

Like the changes in my eyesight, these ideas had slowly built up over time. They were like lenses in a pair of glasses. They did not change the outside world; they changed how I saw it. And I was not aware of the lenses.

When I came into the Fellowship of AA, I realized I had different lenses from my fellow AAs. My new AA friends could read road signs of life that I could see but not read.

Applying the Steps to all my affairs, I replaced the lenses in my attitude glasses. My new attitudes were, "I can learn from this," "I am grateful for God's presence," "The world is unfolding as God would have it," and "God loves me." New lenses to see the world. These are attitudes and beliefs that refocused my perceptions of reality. They bend the information that I process. I no longer feel oppressed or self-centred.

The world did not change, only my perceptions.

I could see life's streetlights and road signs. I navigated life better.

By the way, the new attitude lenses are great, but like physical lenses, they can become fogged and dirty. When that happens, my perceptions are distorted; once again I feel the world is out to get me. That is my reminder to clean my spiritual glasses, to work the Steps.

Who Is Flying the Plane?

I saw a bumper sticker that read, "God is my Co-Pilot."

The owner of the car broadcasted his relationship with God, a relationship that works for him.

But that relationship would not work for me. Not at all.

My bumper sticker would read, "God is my Pilot."

When God is my Pilot, He is running things, and it works well; when I take over, not so much.

The pilot is the senior; the co-pilot is the junior. If God is my co-pilot, I am the pilot; I am in charge. I pick and choose what I will do or not do. I decide if defects should be removed. I set the course and speed for my life.

God is a great co-pilot, but as co-pilot, God is limited to calling out warnings like, "You are flying too low," "You are going in the wrong direction," or "You are running out of fuel."

And He speaks softly; I can easily ignore the advice and exercise my judgment. And when I do that, I often crash land or end up at the wrong airport.

It is much better when He is the pilot flying the plane, and I am the co-pilot. Unlike God, who is quiet as a co-pilot, I am loud and anxious. I shout out my warnings, like, "Are you sure about this?" or "I can't possibly do that," or, "I need some help."

Airplane pilots refer to the pilot in charge as having the "left" seat and more junior co-pilot in the "right" seat. If the plane seems to be in trouble, guaranteed God is in the right seat.

As fast as possible, I should get out of the left seat and let Him take over.

What's Next?

If you haven't read book 1, *GEMS 12-Step Shares, Notes and Thoughts*, you can find it at
the4thdimension.ca/book/gems/
and all major online book retailers.

And book 3, *Still More GEMS, 12-Step Shares, Notes and Thoughts*, available at
the4thdimension.ca/book/still-more-gems/

Get weekly GEMS in your mailbox by signing up for Andy C's newsletter at
the4thdimension.ca/subscribe/

For other books, bookmarks, printables, and more, check out Andy C's eStore at
the4thdimensionca.square.site/

Biography

Andy C. has captured large elements of his sobriety with this book. Many of the lessons portrayed in the stories are from his experiences and observations as a lawyer, social leader and parent.

He was born in small town Ontario, Canada. He sobered up in his third year of law school, November 3, 1977. He graduated from Lakehead University with a Commerce and Finance Degree and then completed a Law Degree at the University of Toronto. He moved to Calgary. He married his life friend and partner, Doreen, and they have two children.

For Andy, not drinking was a first spiritual awakening. He's been blessed with subsequent spiritual awakenings as the result of the practice of the program of Alcoholics Anonymous and good sponsorship.

Andy is active in service work in AA and was instrumental in the foundation and ongoing growth of Simon House in Calgary. He was also a leader in the Lawyers' Assist Program of Alberta, assisting lawyers in crisis often with booze and alcohol. Andy is involved in prodigious 12-step work. He is sponsored, sponsors others, and has a Home Group

Visit Andy C. at
the4thdimension.ca

For more books, blog posts, podcasts,
printable worksheets,
and to subscribe to his weekly newsletter.